Special Clean Eating Edition
MEDITERRANEAN
Diet Cookbook for Beginners

172 Budget-Friendly, Easy, Mouthwatering Recipes for a Healthier and Happier Life

AMBER BOURN

Contents

SEAFOOD 65

VEGETABLE, VEGETARIAN & GRAIN DISHES 75

DESSERTS 91

28-Day Meal Plan   100

Shopping List   100

BONUS   104

INDEX   105

YOUR GUIDE TO THE NEW WAY OF MEDITERRANEAN EATING

How to Adjust the Mediterranean Diet and Go Green

This book offers a refreshing approach to traditional Mediterranean eating patterns, emphasizing sustainable and environmentally friendly choices. It's an excellent resource for beginners who want to improve their health and minimize their environmental impact.

The author adeptly weaves the core principles of the Mediterranean diet—abundant in **fruits**, **vegetables**, **whole grains**, and **healthy fats**—into modern, sustainable practices. The book's emphasis on local and seasonal produce, reduced meat consumption, and alternatives to processed foods offers practical strategies that promote health and sustainability in everyday life.

One of the standout features of this book is its actionable advice on selecting healthy and sustainable seafood. It recognizes the challenges of overfishing and the importance of preserving marine biodiversity. Additionally, including plant-based alternatives reflects a thoughtful consideration of current dietary trends and environmental concerns.

The recipes are straightforward, delicious, and visually appealing. They are accompanied by tips on how to source ingredients sustainably. Whether a vibrant salad or a hearty grain dish, each recipe encourages cooking with whole, unprocessed foods.

In conclusion, "Clean Eating Mediterranean Diet Cookbook for Beginners" is a commendable guide that combines nutritional guidance with environmental stewardship. It's an essential read for anyone looking to adopt a healthier lifestyle while caring for our planet.

What is the green Mediterranean Diet?

The Green Mediterranean diet, a variation of the traditional Mediterranean diet, places a greater emphasis on plant-based foods and less on meat. This dietary shift is not only beneficial for the environment but also for your health. By increasing the intake of specific plant-based components and reducing red meat consumption, this diet modification enhances the already recognized health benefits of the Mediterranean diet. Here's what distinguishes the Green Mediterranean diet:

Key Features of the Green Mediterranean Diet:

Higher Intake of Plant-based Foods:

The diet includes more daily servings of fruits, vegetables, whole grains, and legumes than the traditional Mediterranean diet.

The diet includes more daily servings of fruits, vegetables, whole grains, and legumes than the traditional Mediterranean diet.

Reduced Meat Consumption:

Red meat is strictly limited to decrease the diet's environmental impact and improve heart health. Poultry and fish are still included but in moderation.

Inclusion of Specific Superfoods:

We emphasize foods like walnuts, green tea, and other plant-based protein sources. These additions are rich in antioxidants and phytochemicals, contributing to overall health benefits.

Use of Mankai Duckweed:

The Green Medi diet often highlights Mankai duckweed, a high-protein aquatic plant. It's used as a green shake and is noted for its high protein content, omega-3 fatty acids, iron, B12, vitamins, and minerals.

Sustainable Seafood:

The diet promotes the consumption of sustainable seafood choices to reduce environmental impact and support ocean health.

Minimal Processed Foods and Sugars:
Similar to the traditional version, the Green Mediterranean diet avoids processed foods and added sugars and focuses on whole, natural ingredients.
Health Benefits:
Heart Health: Studies have shown that the Green Mediterranean diet significantly improves heart health metrics, including reductions in cholesterol and blood pressure.
Weight Loss: The high fiber content from increased plant consumption can help manage weight by keeping you fuller for longer.
Reduced Risk of Chronic Diseases: Like its traditional counterpart, the Green Mediterranean diet

Green Med is even better for Your Health

The Green Mediterranean diet takes the well-established health benefits of the traditional Mediterranean diet and enhances them by further emphasizing plant-based foods and reducing meat consumption. Here's why the Green Mediterranean diet could be even better for your health.
The Green Mediterranean diet aligns with contemporary environmental concerns and the latest nutritional science for disease prevention and overall health. It tweaks the traditional Mediterranean diet to include more greens and fewer animal products, making it an appealing choice for those looking to maintain a healthy lifestyle that respects planetary health.

THE BEST ADVICE FOR SHOPPING ON A BUDGET

If you shop hungry, you're much more likely to make impulse purchases, so go after a meal or grab a healthy snack before heading to the store!

Shopping on a budget can be a practical way to manage your finances while enjoying nutritious, satisfying meals. Here are some effective strategies to help you maximize your grocery budget:

Plan Your Meals:
Before you shop, take control and plan your meals for the week. This will help you avoid buying items you don't need and ensure you utilize what you buy, reducing waste. Stick to your shopping list to avoid impulse purchases.

Shop Seasonally:
Purchase fruits and vegetables that are in season. They are generally cheaper and at their peak flavor. This is also a great way to vary your diet throughout the year.

Use Coupons and Loyalty Cards:
Take advantage of discounts, coupons, and store loyalty programs. Many stores offer significant savings through these programs, and digital coupons can often be found on store websites or apps.

Buy in Bulk:
Items like rice, pasta, dried beans, and certain canned goods are often cheaper in bulk. Be sure you have enough storage space and a plan to use these items before expiration.

Choose Generic Brands:
Store or generic brands typically offer the same quality as national brands but at a lower cost. They can be found in nearly every product, from spices and baking ingredients to dairy and frozen foods.

Limit Meat Purchases:
Meat can be expensive. Reducing meat consumption and substituting it with other protein sources like lentils, chickpeas, eggs, or tofu can lower grocery bills and add variety to your diet.

Cook from Scratch:
Prepared and processed foods are usually more expensive than cooking from scratch. However, cooking your own meals can be more economical and healthier, as you can control the ingredients and portions.

Reduce Waste:
Use leftovers creatively and store food properly to extend its shelf life. Freeze surplus fruits and vegetables or make soups, stews, or broths with items nearing expiration.

Shop at Discount Stores:
Explore local discount supermarkets or wholesale clubs where you can find lower prices on many staples.

Look for Sales and Special Offers:
Look in weekly flyers and online for special sales at your local grocery stores. Planning your meals around these deals can lead to significant savings.

Grow Your Own:
Start a small garden with herbs and vegetables. This can be a cost-effective and rewarding way to supplement your grocery shopping, giving you a sense of accomplishment and satisfaction.

Use Everything:
You should utilize all parts of the food you buy. For example, vegetable scraps and meat bones can be used to make stock, and stale bread can be turned into croutons or breadcrumbs. This responsible approach not only saves money but also reduces food waste.

By implementing these strategies, you can make the most of your grocery budget while still enjoying delicious, healthy meals that adhere to the Clean Eating Mediterranean Diet.

BREAKFAST

Crepes with Smoked Salmon & Quick-Pickled Onions

⏰ PREP: **10 mins** 🔍 COOK: **20 mins** 🍽 SERVES: **4**

1 cup all-purpose flour
1 1/2 cups milk
2 large eggs
1/2 teaspoon salt
4 ounces smoked salmon
1/2 cup thinly sliced red onions

1. Combine white vinegar, sugar, and salt in a small bowl. Add thinly sliced onions, ensuring they are fully submerged. Let sit for at least 15 minutes while you prepare the crepes.
2. Place flour, milk, eggs, and salt in a blender. Blend until the mixture is smooth and bubbles form on top, about 30 seconds.
3. Heat a non-stick skillet over medium heat. Pour about 1/4 cup of the crepe batter into the center of the skillet, swirling to spread evenly.
4. Roast for 1 to 2 minutes on each side or until lightly golden. Repeat with the remaining batter.
5. Lay a crepe flat on a plate. Arrange a slice of smoked salmon in the center and top it with a spoonful of pickled onions.
Per serving: Calories: 260 kcal, Protein: 15g, Carbohydrates: 29g, Fats: 9g, Fiber: 1g

Easy Harissa Shakshuka

⏰ PREP: **5 mins** 🔍 COOK: **10 mins** 🍽 SERVES: **4**

2 tablespoons harissa paste
1 can (28 oz) crushed tomatoes
4 large eggs
1 tablespoon olive oil
Salt and pepper, to taste
Fresh parsley or cilantro for garnish

1. In a large skillet, heat olive oil over medium heat. Stir in the harissa paste quickly, then pour in the crushed tomatoes—season with salt and pepper.
2. Let the sauce simmer for about 10 minutes until it thickens slightly.
3. With a spoon, make wells in the tomato sauce. Crack an egg into each well.
4. Cover the skillet and let the eggs cook for about 5 minutes, or until the whites are set but the yolks are still runny.
5. Remove from heat and sprinkle chopped parsley or cilantro over the top for freshness.
6. Serve hot, ideally with a slice of crusty bread to dip into the sauce and egg.
Per serving: Calories: 180 kcal, Protein: 10g, Carbohydrates: 10g, Fats: 11g, Fiber: 2g, Cholesterol: 164 mg, Sodium: 300 mg

Salmon Bagel Salad with Lemon Buttermilk Dressing

🕐 PREP: **10 mins** 🔍 COOK: **0 mins** 🍽 SERVES: **4**

4 whole-grain bagels torn into bite-sized pieces
8 ounces smoked salmon
2 cups arugula
1/2 cup buttermilk
2 tablespoons lemon juice
1 tablespoon fresh chives, finely chopped

1. Combine buttermilk, lemon juice, and chopped chives in a small bowl. Whisk together until smooth.
2. Spread the torn bagel pieces on a baking sheet and toast under a broiler or in a toaster oven until crispy and golden. Let cool.
3. Toss the arugula and crispy bagel pieces in a large mixing bowl with half of the dressing. Arrange on plates.
4. Layer slices of smoked salmon over the dressed salad.
5. Drizzle the remaining dressing over the salmon and garnish with additional chives if desired.
6. Serve immediately, ensuring the bagel pieces retain their crunch for a pleasant texture contrast to the soft salmon and fresh arugula.

Per serving: Calories: 350 kcal, Protein: 24g, Carbohydrates: 37g, Fats: 10g, Fiber: 5g, Sodium: 670 mg

Blueberry Cheesecake Smoothie

🕐 PREP: **10 mins** 🔍 COOK: **0 mins** 🍽 SERVES: **4**

1 cup frozen blueberries
1/2 cup Greek yogurt (plain)
1/4 cup rolled oats
2 tablespoons cream cheese (preferably light or vegan)
1 tablespoon honey or maple syrup (adjust to taste)
1 cup unsweetened almond milk

1. Combine the frozen blueberries, Greek yogurt, rolled oats, cream cheese, honey or maple syrup, and almond milk in a blender.
2. Blend on high until smooth and creamy, ensuring the oats and blueberries are fully incorporated.
3. If the smoothie is too thick, add more almond milk and blend again to reach your desired consistency.
4. Pour the smoothie into glasses. For a touch of elegance, garnish with a few whole blueberries or a mint leaf.
5. Enjoy this nutritious smoothie as a breakfast treat or a refreshing afternoon snack.

Per serving: Calories: 180 kcal, Protein: 6 g, Carbohydrates: 27 g, Fats: 5 g, Fiber: 3 g, Cholesterol: 15 mg, Sodium: 120 mg

Grain-Free Chicken & Vegetable Quiche

⏰ PREP: **10 mins** ◎ COOK: **30 mins** 🍽 SERVES: **4**

4 large eggs
1 cup cooked chicken breast, diced
1 cup fresh spinach, chopped
1/2 cup cherry tomatoes, halved
1/2 cup almond milk
Salt and pepper, to taste

1. Preheat your oven to 375°F (190°C).
2. Whisk the eggs and almond milk together in a large mixing bowl until well combined.
3. Stir in the diced chicken, chopped spinach, and cherry tomatoes. Season with salt and pepper to taste.
4. Grease a pie dish with olive oil or use a non-stick spray. Pour the egg and vegetable mixture into the pie dish.
5. Place in the preheated oven and bake for 35 minutes until the center is set and the top is golden.
6. Let the quiche cool for a few minutes before slicing.

Per serving: Calories: 220 kcal, Protein: 23 g, Carbohydrates: 4 g, Fats: 12 g, Fiber: 1 g, Cholesterol: 215 mg, Sodium: 220 mg

Pumpkin and Amaretto Biscuit Pudding

⏰ PREP: **20 mins** ◎ COOK: **1 hour** 🍽 SERVES: **8**

1-quart milk, 3 lb pumpkin, peeled and cubed
6 Amaretto biscuits, crushed
1/2 cup sugar, 3 large eggs
1/4 cup unsalted butter, melted
1/2 cup bread crumbs
1 teaspoon vanilla extract
1/2 teaspoon ground cinnamon

1. In a large pot, boil the cubed pumpkin in water until tender, about 15-20 mins. Drain well and mash until smooth.
2. Preheat your oven to 350°F (175°C).
3. Whisk together the milk, eggs, sugar, melted butter, vanilla extract, cinnamon, nutmeg, and salt in a mixing bowl. Stir in the mashed pumpkin.
4. Fold in the crushed Amaretto biscuits and bread crumbs into the pumpkin mixture.
5. Pour the mixture into a buttered baking dish. Bake in the preheated oven for about 1 hour
6. Allow the pudding to cool to room temperature, then refrigerate for at least 2 hours before serving.

Per serving: Calories: 320 kcal, Protein: 7g, Carbohydrates: 45g, Fats: 12g, Fiber: 3g, Cholesterol: 95 mg, Sodium: 180 mg

Trout Breakfast Salad with Creamy Dill Dressing

⏰ PREP: **10 mins** ◎ COOK: **0 mins** 🍽 SERVES: **4**

2 cups baby spinach
4 ounces smoked trout, flaked
1/4 cup Greek yogurt
2 tablespoons fresh dill, finely chopped
1 tablespoon lemon juice
Salt and pepper, to taste

1. Combine Greek yogurt, fresh dill, and lemon juice in a small bowl. Whisk until smooth—season with salt and pepper to taste.
2. Place the baby spinach in a large salad bowl. Gently lay the flaked smoked trout over the spinach.
3. Evenly drizzle the creamy dill dressing over the salad. Toss lightly to mix the ingredients well.
4. Serve immediately, perfect for a refreshing and hearty breakfast.
Per serving: Calories: 180 kcal, Protein: 18 g, Carbohydrates: 4 g, Fats: 10 g, Fiber: 2 g, Cholesterol: 30 mg, Sodium: 200 mg

Med Salad with Chickpeas & Herbed Vinaigrette

⏰ PREP: **10 mins** ◎ COOK: **15 mins** 🍽 SERVES: **8**

1 can (15 oz) chickpeas, drained, rinsed, and dried
4 cups mixed salad greens (like romaine, arugula, and spinach)
1/2 cup cherry tomatoes, halved
1/4 cup olive oil
2 tablespoons lemon juice
1 tablespoon mixed dried herbs

1. Preheat your oven to 400°F (200°C).
2. Spread the chickpeas on a baking sheet and drizzle with 1 tablespoon of olive oil.
3. Roast in the oven for 15 minutes or until crispy and golden.
4. In a small bowl, whisk together the remaining olive oil, lemon juice, and dried herbs. Season with salt and pepper to taste.
5. In a large salad bowl, combine the mixed greens, cherry tomatoes, and crispy chickpeas.
6. Drizzle the herbed vinaigrette over the salad and toss well to coat.
7. Divide the salad among plates and serve immediately, ensuring the chickpeas retain their crunch for a pleasant texture contrast.
Per serving: Calories: 240 kcal, Protein: 7 g, Carbohydrates: 18 g, Fats: 16 g, Fiber: 5 g, Cholesterol: 0 mg, Sodium: 200 mgum: 180 mg

Fruit & Nut Couscous

🕐 PREP: **5 mins** 🔍 COOK: **15 mins** 🍽 SERVES: **4**

1 cup couscous
1 1/4 cups water or any light stock (for cooking the couscous)
1/2 cup mixed dried fruits (such as apricots, raisins, cranberries, chopped)
1/2 cup mixed nuts (such as almonds, walnuts, and pecans, roughly chopped)
1/2 teaspoon ground cinnamon
2 tablespoons honey

1. Bring the water or stock and a pinch of salt to a boil in a medium saucepan. Stir in the couscous, then cover and remove from heat. Let it sit for about 5 minutes until the liquid is absorbed and the couscous is fluffy.
2. Fluff the cooked couscous with a fork to separate the grains. Sprinkle the ground cinnamon over the couscous and mix it through evenly.
3. Stir the dried fruits and nuts into the couscous while still warm. The heat helps release the dried fruits' flavors and slightly toast the nuts.
4. Drizzle honey over the couscous mixture and stir well to coat all ingredients. Serve warm or allow to cool to room temperature, depending on preference.
Per serving: Calories: 300 kcal, Protein: 6 g, Carbohydrates: 50 g, Fats: 8 g, Fiber: 4 g, Sodium: 15 mg

Cucumber & Herb Yogurt Salad

🕐 PREP: **10 mins** 🔍 COOK: **0 mins** 🍽 SERVES: **4**

2 cups Greek yogurt
1 large cucumber, diced
2 tablespoons fresh dill, finely chopped
2 tablespoons fresh mint, finely chopped
1 clove garlic, minced
Salt and pepper, to taste

1. Peel the cucumber and dice it into small cubes. Finely chop the fresh dill and mint. Mince the garlic clove.
2. Combine the Greek yogurt, diced cucumber, chopped dill, mint, and minced garlic in a large mixing bowl. Stir until all the ingredients are well combined. Season with salt and pepper to taste.
3. Cover the salad and refrigerate for about 30 minutes to allow the flavors to meld.
4. Serve chilled as a refreshing side dish or appetizer.
Per serving: Calories: 90, Protein: 5g, Carbohydrates: 6g, Fat: 4g, Fiber: 1g, Cholesterol: 10mg, Sodium: 50mg

Muesli with Skyr

⏰ PREP: **10 mins** 🍳 COOK: **0 mins** 🍽 SERVES: **4**

1 cup mixed grains (such as oats, barley, and rye flakes)
1/4 cup mixed nuts (such as almonds, walnuts, and hazelnuts),
chopped
1/4 cup mixed seeds (such as sunflower seeds and pumpkin seeds)
1/4 cup dried fruits (such as raisins, apricots, and cranberries),
chopped
1 1/2 cups Icelandic skyr yogurt
Optional: Honey or maple syrup for sweetness

1. In a large bowl, mix the grains, nuts, seeds, and dried fruits. Add enough water to cover the mixture, stirring well.
2. Cover the bowl with plastic wrap or a lid and refrigerate overnight. This allows the grains to soften and the flavors to meld together.
3. Stir the mixture to refresh it the following day. Spoon into bowls and top each serving with a generous dollop of skyr yogurt.
4. If desired, drizzle honey or maple syrup over the top for added sweetness.
5. Serve immediately for a refreshing and filling breakfast.

Per serving: Calories: 350 kcal, Protein: 20 g, Carbohydrates: 45 g, Fat: 10 g, Fiber: 6 g, Cholesterol: 10 mg, Sodium: 50 mg

Mediterranean Breakfast Wraps

⏰ PREP: **5 mins** 🍳 COOK: **10 mins** 🍽 SERVES: **4**

4 whole-grain wraps
6 large eggs, beaten
1/2 cup Kalamata olives, chopped
1 medium tomato, diced
1 cucumber, diced
1/2 cup tzatziki sauce

1. Heat a non-stick skillet over medium heat and add some olive oil.
2. Pour the beaten eggs into the skillet. Stir gently and cook until the eggs are softly scrambled about 3-4 minutes. Season with salt and pepper to taste. Remove from heat and set aside.
3. While the eggs are cooking, chop the tomatoes, cucumbers, and olives into small pieces.
4. Lay out the whole-grain wraps on a clean surface. Divide the scrambled eggs evenly among the wraps.
5. Top each wrap with equal amounts of chopped tomatoes, cucumbers, and olives. Add a generous dollop of tzatziki sauce over the top of the fillings.
6. Carefully fold the sides of each wrap inward and then roll them up tightly to secure the fillings.
7. Cut each wrap in half diagonally and serve immediately.

Per serving: Calories: 300 kcal, Protein: 15 g, Carbohydrates: 20 g, Fats: 15 g, Fiber: 4 g, Cholesterol: 280 mg, Sodium: 400 mg

Whole-Grain Pancakes with Fruit Compote

⏰ PREP: **10 mins** 🔍 COOK: **30 mins** 🍽️ SERVES: **4**

Whole-wheat flour: 1 cup
Baking Powder: 2 teaspoons
Milk: 1 cup (can use any kind, including non-dairy alternatives)
Egg: 1 large
Honey: 2 tablespoons
Butter or Coconut Oil: For cooking
Mixed Berries (fresh or frozen): 2 cups , Orange Juice: ¼ cup

1. In a large bowl, combine the whole-wheat flour and baking powder.
2. In another bowl, whisk together the milk, egg, and honey. Let the batter sit for a few minutes to thicken slightly.
3. Heat a non-stick skillet or griddle over medium heat and brush with butter or coconut oil.
4. Pour ¼ cup of batter for each pancake onto the hot skillet. Roast until bubbles form on the surface and the edges look set about 2 minutes.
5. Combine the berries, orange juice, and honey in a small saucepan.
6. Bring to a simmer over medium heat and cook for about 10 minutes, until the fruits break down.

Per serving: Calories: 280 kcal, Protein: 7 g, Carbohydrates: 49 g, Fats: 6 g, Fiber: 6 g, Sodium: 300 mg

Eggplant & Yogurt Parfait

⏰ PREP: **15 mins** 🔍 COOK: **25 mins** 🍽️ SERVES: **4**

1 large eggplant, cut into small cubes
2 cups Greek yogurt
1/4 cup mixed nuts (walnuts, almonds), chopped
2 tablespoons honey, plus extra for drizzling
1 tablespoon olive oil
Salt, to taste

1. Preheat your oven to 400°F (200°C). Toss the cubed eggplant with olive oil and a pinch of salt. Spread on a baking sheet in a single layer.
2. Roast in the oven for 25-30 minutes or until the eggplant is golden and tender. Allow to cool slightly.
3. In clear serving glasses, begin by layering a spoonful of Greek yogurt at the bottom. Add a layer of roasted eggplant. Sprinkle a layer of chopped nuts and drizzle some honey.
4. Repeat the layering process until the glasses are filled, finishing with a layer of Greek yogurt on top.
5. Drizzle with more honey and garnish with a few more chopped nuts for extra crunch.
6. Chill in the refrigerator for 10 minutes before serving to allow the flavors to meld together.

Per serving: Calories: 280 kcal, Protein: 15 g, Carbohydrates: 26 g, Fats: 15 g, Fiber: 5 g, Cholesterol: 10 mg, Sodium: 150 mg

Cottage Cheese with Sliced Peaches and Fresh Mint

🕐 PREP: **5 mins**   ⏲ COOK: **0 mins**   🍽 SERVES: **4**

1 cup cottage cheese
2 fresh peaches, sliced
2 tablespoons fresh mint, chopped
1 tablespoon honey

1. Wash the peaches thoroughly under running water. Slice them into even pieces, removing the pit. Rinse and chop the fresh mint leaves finely.
2. Scoop the cottage cheese into serving bowls.
Arrange the sliced peaches attractively on top of the cottage cheese.
3. Sprinkle the chopped mint over the peaches and cottage cheese.
4.Drizzle honey evenly over each serving for a touch of natural sweetness.
5. Serve immediately and enjoy this nutritious, flavorful breakfast.
Per serving: Calories: 180 kcal, Protein: 13 g, Carbohydrates: 20 g, Fats: 5 g, Fiber: 2 g, Cholesterol: 10 mg, Sodium: 200 mg

Artichok & Ricotta Whole-Grain Toast

🕐 PREP: **10 mins**   ⏲ COOK: **5 mins**   🍽 SERVES: **4**

2 slices whole-grain bread
1/2 cup ricotta cheese
4 marinated artichoke hearts, chopped
Fresh herbs (such as basil, parsley, or chives), chopped
Salt and pepper, to taste

1. Preheat your oven's broiler or use a toaster to toast the whole-grain bread slices until they are golden and crispy.
2. Mix the ricotta cheese with a pinch of salt and pepper in a small bowl. Stir until smooth.
3. Spread a generous amount of the seasoned ricotta cheese on each slice of toasted bread. Top evenly with the chopped marinated artichoke hearts.
4. Sprinkle the chopped fresh herbs over the top for a flavor and a touch of color.
5. Serve immediately while the toast is still warm.
Per serving: Calories: 210, Protein: 12 g, Carbohydrates: 22 g, Fat: 9 g, Fiber: 4 g, Cholesterol: 31 mg, Sodium: 390 mg

Grilled Tomato and Halloumi Skewers

⏰ PREP: **10 mins**   🍳 COOK: **30 mins**   🍽 SERVES: **4**

8 oz halloumi cheese, cut into 1-inch cubes
16 cherry tomatoes
1/4 cup balsamic vinegar
2 tablespoons olive oil
Salt and freshly ground black pepper to taste
Fresh basil leaves, for garnish (optional)

1. Preheat your grill to medium-high heat, or prepare a pan on the stove.
2. Bring the balsamic vinegar to a boil over medium heat in a small saucepan. 3. Reduce the heat and simmer until the vinegar thickens, reducing to about half its original volume, approximately 10 minutes.
4. Set aside to cool; it will continue to thicken as it cools.
5. Thread the halloumi cubes and cherry tomatoes alternately onto skewers.
6. Brush the skewers lightly with olive oil and season with salt and pepper.
7. Grill the skewers, turning occasionally, about 8-10 minutes.
8. Drizzle the skewers with the balsamic reduction. Garnish with fresh basil leaves if desired.

Per serving: Calories: 250 kcal, Protein: 12 g, Carbohydrates: 8 g, Fat: 19 g, Fiber: 1 g, Cholesterol: 30 mg, Sodium: 600 mg

Mediterranean Breakfast Salad

⏰ PREP: **5 mins**   🍳 COOK: **15 mins**   🍽 SERVES: **4**

2 cups arugula
1/2 cup cherry tomatoes, halved
1/2 cucumber, sliced
1/4 cup Kalamata olives, pitted
2 eggs
2 tablespoons olive oil
Juice of 1 lemon

1. Whisk together the olive oil, lemon juice, salt, and pepper in a small bowl. Set aside.
2. Bring a pot of water to a simmer. Crack each egg into a small cup, then gently slide the eggs into the simmering water one at a time. Cook for 3 to 4 minutes until the whites are set, but the yolks remain runny. Remove with a slotted spoon and drain on a paper towel.
3. Combine the arugula, cherry tomatoes, cucumber slices, and olives in a large salad bowl. Drizzle the dressing over the salad and toss gently to coat everything evenly.
4. Divide the salad between two plates and top each with a poached egg.

Per serving: Calories: 250 kcal, Protein: 8 g, Carbohydrates: 8 g, Fats: 21 g, Fiber: 3 g, Cholesterol: 185 mg, Sodium: 300 mg

Whole-Grain Breakfast Pizza

⏰ PREP: **10 mins** ⊘ COOK: **15 mins** 🍽 SERVES: **4**

2 small whole-grain pizza bases (about 6 inches each)
1/2 cup tomato sauce (preferably low sodium)
1/2 cup low-fat mozzarella cheese, shredded
4 fresh basil leaves, torn
2 large eggs
Optional: Red pepper flakes, salt, and freshly ground black pepper

1. Preheat your oven to 425°F (220°C).
2. Place the whole-grain pizza bases on a baking sheet.
3. Add Toppings: Spread tomato sauce evenly over each pizza base. Sprinkle with low-fat mozzarella cheese and arrange basil leaves on top.
4. Carefully crack an egg in the center of each pizza.
5. Optionally, sprinkle with red pepper flakes, salt, and black pepper.
6. Place the pizzas in the oven and bake for 12-15 minutes, or until the egg whites are set but the yolks are still slightly runny and the edges of the pizza are crispy.
7. Remove from the oven, let cool for a minute, and serve hot.

Per serving: Calories: 320 kcal, Protein: 18 g, Carbohydrates: 36 g, Fats: 12 g, Fiber: 6 g, Cholesterol: 190 mg, Sodium: 400 mg, Potassium: 200

Quinoa and Chia Porridge

⏰ PREP: **5 mins** ⊘ COOK: **15 mins** 🍽 SERVES: **4**

1/2 cup quinoa, rinsed
2 tablespoons chia seeds
2 cups unsweetened almond milk
1/2 teaspoon ground cinnamon
1 cup fresh berries (such as blueberries, raspberries, or sliced strawberries)

1. Combine the quinoa and almond milk in a small saucepan. Bring to a boil over medium-high heat. Reduce heat to low, cover, and simmer for 10-15 minutes until the quinoa is tender and the liquid is mostly absorbed.
2. Stir in the chia seeds and cinnamon, and cook for 5 minutes or until the mixture thickens to a porridge-like consistency.
3. While cooking the porridge, rinse the fresh berries and set aside.
4. Spoon the porridge into bowls and top with fresh berries.
5. Drizzle with a bit of honey or maple syrup if a sweeter taste is desired.
6. Add a sprinkle of nuts or seeds for added texture and nutrients.

Per serving: Calories: 280 kcal, Protein: 8 g, Carbohydrates: 42 g, Fats: 9 g, Fiber: 10 g, Sodium: 80 mg, Potassium: 200 mg

Roasted Pepper and Goat Cheese Bruschetta

🕐 PREP: **10 mins** ◎ COOK: **15 mins** 🍽 SERVES: **4**

4 whole-grain baguettes, sliced
2 large bell peppers (preferably red and yellow for color)
100g goat cheese, softened
1 tablespoon olive oil
Fresh basil leaves for garnish
Salt and pepper, to taste

1. Preheat your oven to 400°F (200°C).
2. Slice the bell peppers into strips, removing the seeds and membranes.
3. Toss the pepper strips with olive oil, salt, and pepper. Spread them on a baking sheet and roast in the oven for about 15 minutes or until they are soft and slightly charred.
4. While the peppers are roasting, place the baguette slices on a baking tray and toast in the oven for about 5 minutes until just crisp.
5. Spread a generous amount of goat cheese on each slice of toasted baguette. 6. Top with a few roasted pepper strips. Garnish each bruschetta with a fresh basil leaf.

Per serving: Calories: 150 kcal, Protein: 5 g, Carbohydrates: 18 g, Fats: 7 g, Fiber: 3 g, Cholesterol: 10 mg, Sodium: 200 mg

Tortilla Española (Spanish Omelette)

🕐 PREP: **15 mins** ◎ COOK: **25 mins** 🍽 SERVES: **4**

Potatoes: 3 medium, peeled and thinly sliced
Onion: 1 large, thinly sliced
Eggs: 6 large
Olive Oil: For frying
Salt: To taste

1. Peel and thinly slice the potatoes. Similarly, thinly slice the onion.
2. Heat a generous amount of olive oil in a non-stick frying pan over medium heat.
3. Add the sliced potatoes and onions to the pan, seasoning with salt. Lower the heat and cook gently, partially covered, for about 20 minutes, stirring occasionally, until the potatoes are tender but not browned.
4. While the potatoes and onions cook, crack the eggs into a large bowl and beat them with a pinch of salt.
5. When the potatoes and onions are cooked, drain them from the oil (you can save them for another use) and add them to the beaten eggs. Mix gently and let sit for about 5 minutes.
6. Clean and heat the same pan with reserved olive oil over medium heat. Pour the potato and egg mixture into the pan, spreading evenly. Cook for about 5 minutes or until the bottom is lightly browned and set.
7. Place a large plate over the pan and carefully invert the omelet onto the plate. Slide the omelet back into the pan with the uncooked side down. Cook for another 4-5 minutes.

Per serving: Calories: 240 kcal, Protein: 8 g, Carbohydrates: 20 g, Fats: 14 g, Fiber: 2 g, Cholesterol:

Simplified Spinach & Feta Phyllo Pie

⏰ PREP: **10 mins** 🍳 COOK: **40 mins** 🍽️ SERVES: **4**

Phyllo Dough: 10 sheets
Spinach: 16 oz (450 g), fresh or frozen (thawed and well-drained)
Feta Cheese: 200 g, crumbled.
Eggs: 3 large, beaten
Olive Oil: For brushing
Salt and Pepper: To taste

1. Preheat your oven to 375°F (190°C).
Brush a 9-inch round baking pan with olive oil.
2. If using fresh spinach, blanch quickly in boiling water, then drain and squeeze out excess water. If using frozen, ensure it's thoroughly drained.
3. Combine the spinach, crumbled feta, and beaten eggs in a mixing bowl—season with salt and pepper to taste.
4. Place one sheet of phyllo in the pan, brushing lightly with olive oil. Repeat with four more sheets, placing each at different angles to cover the pan thoroughly. Spread the spinach mixture over the phyllo. Cover with the remaining phyllo sheets, brush each with olive oil, and tuck in the edges to seal.
5. Bake for about 40 minutes until the phyllo is golden brown and crisp.

Per serving: Calories: 290 kcal, Protein: 11 g, Carbohydrates: 24 g, Fats: 18 g, Fiber: 2 g, Cholesterol: 95 mg, Sodium: 460 mg

Mediterranean Omelette

⏰ PREP: **10 mins** 🍳 COOK: **10 mins** 🍽️ SERVES: **1**

Eggs: 3 large
Fresh Spinach: 1 cup, roughly chopped
Cherry Tomatoes: ½ cup, halved
Black Olives: ¼ cup, pitted and sliced
Feta Cheese: ¼ cup, crumbled
Olive Oil: 1 tablespoon
Salt and Pepper: To taste

1. Wash and chop the spinach. Halve the cherry tomatoes and slice the olives.
2. Crack the eggs in a mixing bowl and season with salt and pepper. Beat them until fully mixed.
3. Heat olive oil in a non-stick skillet over medium heat. Add the spinach and tomatoes, cooking for 1-2 minutes until the spinach wilts and tomatoes are slightly softened.
4. Pour the beaten eggs evenly over the vegetables in the skillet. Sprinkle the sliced olives and crumbled feta cheese over the top.
5. Let the eggs cook undisturbed for a few minutes until the edges lift from the skillet. Using a spatula, gently lift the edges while tilting the pan to allow the uncooked egg to flow underneath.
6. Once the bottom is set and the top is still slightly runny, fold the omelet in half or roll it up in the pan.

Per serving: Calories: 400 kcal, Protein: 24 g, Carbohydrates: 8 g, Fats: 32 g, Fiber: 2 g, Cholesterol:

Green Morning Smoothie

⏰ PREP: **5 mins** ⏲ COOK: **5 mins** 🍽 SERVES: **4**

Spinach: 2 cups, fresh
Bananas: 2 large, sliced and frozen
Apple: 1 large, cored and cut into chunks
Lemon Juice: From 1 lemon
Water: 2 cups (adjust for desired consistency)
Ice Cubes: Optional for chilling

1. Ensure the bananas are sliced and frozen beforehand to give the smoothie a creamier texture.
2. Core and chunk the apple. You can leave the skin on for extra nutrients.
3. Add the fresh spinach, frozen banana slices, apple chunks, and lemon juice in your blender. Pour in the water. Use less for a thicker smoothie or more for a thinner consistency. If desired, add ice cubes for an extra cold smoothie.
4. Blend on high until all the ingredients are thoroughly combined, and the texture is smooth.

Per serving: Calories: 120 kcal, Protein: 2 g, Carbohydrates: 30 g, Fats: 0.5 g, Fiber: 4 g

Earthy Granola

⏰ PREP: **10 mins** ⏲ COOK: **30 mins** 🍽 SERVES: **4**

Old-Fashioned Oats: 3 cups
Raw Almonds: 1 cup, coarsely chopped
Pumpkin Seeds: 1/2 cup
Maple Syrup: 1/3 cup (can adjust for desired sweetness)
Coconut Oil: 1/4 cup, melted
Cinnamon: 1 teaspoon
1/4 teaspoon ground nutmeg

1. Preheat your oven to 300°F (150°C). Line a baking sheet with parchment paper to prevent sticking.
2. Combine the oats, almonds, and pumpkin seeds in a mixing bowl. Whisk together the melted coconut oil, maple syrup, and cinnamon in a separate small bowl.
3. Pour the wet ingredients over the oat mixture and stir until well-coated.
4. Spread the granola mixture evenly onto the prepared baking sheet.
5. Bake in the oven for 30 minutes, stirring halfway through to ensure even cooking and prevent burning.
6. Remove the granola from the oven and let it cool completely on the baking sheet. The granola will crisp up as it cools.

Per serving: Calories: 220 kcal, Protein: 6 g, Carbohydrates: 26 g, Fats: 12 g, Fiber: 4 g, Sodium: 5 mg

SNACKS & SIDES

Lemon Cashew Dip

⏰ PREP: **10 mins** ◎ COOK: **10 mins** 🍽 SERVES: **4**

Raw Cashews: 1 cup, soaked for 4 hours or overnight in water
Lemon Juice: From 1-2 lemons (about ¼ cup)
Lemon Zest: 1 teaspoon
Garlic: 1 clove, minced
Olive Oil: 2 tablespoons
Water: ¼ cup, or as needed for desired consistency1/4 teaspoon ground nutmeg

1. Soak the cashews in water for at least 4 hours or overnight. This softens them and makes them easier to blend into a creamy texture. Drain and rinse the cashews before using.
2. Combine the soaked and drained cashews, lemon juice, lemon zest, minced garlic, and olive oil in a blender or food processor. Blend on high until smooth and creamy. Gradually add water and a tablespoon until the dip reaches your desired consistency. It should be smooth but not too runny.
3. Taste the dip and add salt to taste. If you want more tanginess, adjust the lemon juice or zest.
4. Serve immediately, or store in an airtight container in the refrigera2or for up to a week. The flavors will continue to meld and develop as the dip chills.

Per serving: Calories: 70 kcal, Protein: 2 g, Carbohydrates: 4 g, Fats: 5 g, Fiber: 0.5 g

Roasted Squash & Sweet Potatoes

⏰ PREP: **10 mins** ◎ COOK: **25 mins** 🍽 SERVES: **4**

Butternut Squash: 1 medium, peeled, seeded, and cubed (about 2 cups)
Sweet Potatoes: 2 large, peeled and cubed (about 2 cups)
Olive Oil: 2 tablespoons
Salt: To taste
Pepper: To taste
Optional Seasonings: Paprika, cinnamon, or herbs such as rosemary or thyme (depending on your preference)

1. Preheat your oven to 425°F (220°C). This high temperature is ideal for roasting, as it will help caramelize the outside of the vegetables while keeping the inside tender.
2. Peel and cube the butternut squash and sweet potatoes, trying to cut them into roughly equal-sized pieces for even cooking.
3. Toss the cubed squash and sweet potatoes in a large mixing bowl with olive oil, salt, and pepper. Add optional seasonings like paprika, cinnamon, or herbs now and toss well to coat.
4. Spread the seasoned vegetables in a single layer on a large baking sheet. Make sure they have enough space; if they are too crowded, they will steam rather than roast, which could make them soggy.
5. Roast in the preheated oven for 25-30 minutes, stirring halfway through the cooking time to ensure even browning. The vegetables are done when they are golden brown on die edges and tender when pierced with a fork.

Per serving: Calories: 200 kcal, Protein: 2 g, Carbohydrates: 34 g, Fats: 7 g, Fiber: 6 g

Stuffed Mini Bell Peppers with Serrano Ham & Cheese

⏰ PREP: **20 mins** ◎ COOK: **10 mins** 🍽 SERVES: **6**

Mini Bell Peppers: 12, halved lengthwise and seeded.
Serrano Ham: 12 thin slices, cut to fit the peppers
Cream Cheese: 4 ounces, softened.
Manchego Cheese: 1/2 cup, grated
Green Onions: 2 tablespoons, finely chopped
Black Pepper: To taste

1. Preheat your oven to 375°F (190°C). This moderate temperature allows the peppers to cook without burning the delicate ham.
2. Wash the mini bell peppers, halve them lengthwise, and remove the seeds and membranes. This creates little boats ready to be stuffed.
3. Combine the softened cream cheese, grated Manchego cheese, and chopped green onions in a mixing bowl. Season with black pepper and mix until well combined. Adjust the seasoning to taste.
4. Fill each pepper half with the cheese mixture. For neater filling, use a small spoon or a piping bag without a tip.
5. Place a small piece of Serrano ham on each stuffed pepper, pressing lightly to adhere to the cheese.
6. Arrange the stuffed peppers on a baking sheet. Ensure they are open enough to allow even cooking.
7. Bake in the oven for about 10 minutes until the peppers are tender and the cheese is bubbly.

Per serving: Calories: 60 kcal, Protein: 3 g, Carbohydrates: 2 g, Fats: 4.5 g, Fiber: 0.5 g

Toasted Rosemary Marcona Almonds

⏰ PREP: **5 mins** ◎ COOK: **15 mins** 🍽 SERVES: **4**

Marcona Almonds: 2 cups
Fresh Rosemary: 2 tablespoons, finely chopped
Olive Oil: 1 tablespoon
Sea Salt: 1/2 teaspoon, or to taste
Black Pepper: A pinch (optional)
1/4 teaspoon ground nutmeg

1. Preheat your oven to 350°F (175°C). This temperature will gently toast the almonds without burning them.
2. Toss the Marcona almonds with olive oil in a mixing bowl until they are evenly coated. This helps the rosemary and seasonings stick to the almonds.
3. Add the finely chopped fresh rosemary, sea salt, and a pinch of black pepper to the almonds. Toss again to ensure all the almonds are evenly coated with the herbs and seasonings.
4. Spread the almonds out in a single layer on a baking sheet. Make sure they are not overcrowded to ensure even toasting.
5. Place in the preheated oven and toast for about 10-12 minutes, stirring halfway through to promote even browning and prevent any from burning.
6. Remove the almonds from the oven and let them cool on the baking sheet for a few minutes. They will continue to crisp up as they cool. Taste and adjust the seasoning, adding more salt or pepper as desired.

Per serving: Calories: 220 kcal, Protein: 6 g, Carbohydrates: 6 g, Fats: 20 g, Fiber: 3 g

White Bean & Roasted Red Pepper Dip

⏰ PREP: **10 mins** 🔍 COOK: **25 mins** 🍽 SERVES: **4**

Canned White Beans: 1 can (15 ounces), rinsed and drained
Roasted Red Peppers: 1 cup, chopped
Garlic: 1 clove, minced
Lemon Juice: 2 tablespoons
Olive Oil: 2 tablespoons
Salt and Pepper: To taste
Paprika or Smoked Paprika: ½ teaspoon, for garnish

1. Preheat your oven to 450°F (230°C). Halve the red peppers, remove the seeds and stems, flatten them on a baking sheet, and skin side up. Roast in the oven until the skins blister and blacken, about 20-25 minutes. Remove from the oven, place in a bowl, and cover with plastic wrap for 10 minutes. Then, peel away the skins and chop the flesh.

2. In the bowl of a food processor, combine the rinsed white beans, chopped roasted red peppers, minced garlic, lemon juice, olive oil. Process until smooth. Season with salt and pepper to taste.

3. Add olive oil or water to reach your desired consistency.

4. Taste and adjust the seasoning, possibly adding more lemon juice or salt.

Per serving: Calories: 100 kcal, Protein: 4 g, Carbohydrates: 12 g, Fats: 4 g, Fiber: 3 g

Fruit & Oat Salad with Crispy Prosciutto

⏰ PREP: **10 mins** 🔍 COOK: **10 mins** 🍽 SERVES: **6**

Old-Fashioned Oats: 1 cup, cooked and cooled
Mixed Fresh Fruits: 2 cups (such as sliced strawberries, blue-berries, sliced peaches, and apples)
Prosciutto: 4 slices
Honey: 2 tablespoons
Lemon Juice: 1 tablespoon
Fresh Mint: A few sprigs, chopped

1. If baking, preheat your oven to 375°F (190°C) or heat a non-stick skillet over medium heat. Place the prosciutto slices on a lined baking sheet and bake for about 10 minutes or until crispy. For pan frying, Cook the prosciutto slices in the skillet until crispy, about 2-3 minutes per side. Once cooked, transfer to a paper towel to drain and cool. Break into small pieces once cooled.

2. Combine the cooked and cooled oats in a large mixing bowl with the mixed fresh fruits.

3. Drizzle with honey and lemon juice and toss gently to combine. Add the chopped mint and a drizzle of olive oil, and season with a pinch of salt and pepper to taste.

4. If using mixed greens, lay them as a base on each serving plate. Spoon the oat and fruit mixture over the greens. Sprinkle the crispy prosciutto pieces over the top.

Per serving: Calories: 250 kcal, Protein: 6 g, Carbohydrates: 38 g, Fats: 8 g, Fiber: 4 g

Greek Yogurt and Honey Dip

⏰ PREP: **5 mins** ◎ COOK: **5 mins** 🍽 SERVES: **6**

Greek Yogurt: 1 cup (use full-fat for a richer flavor or non-fat for a lighter version)
Honey: 2 tablespoons, plus extra for drizzling
Vanilla Extract: 1/2 teaspoon (optional, for added depth of flavor)

1. Combine the Greek yogurt, honey, and vanilla extract in a mixing bowl. Stir until well combined and smooth. The vanilla enhances th1 depth of the yogurt's flavor but is optional based on your taste preference.
2. Transfer the dip to a serving bowl. Drizzle extra honey over the top and sprinkle a pinch of cinnamon for added flavor and a beautiful presentation.
3. Serve the dip with a variety of fresh fruits, such as apple slices, banana rounds, strawberries, or blueberries. It also pairs wonderfully with nuts, granola, pancakes, or waffles.

Per serving: Calories: 90 kcal, Protein: 5 g, Carbohydrates: 12 g, Sodium: Low

Melon, Prosciutto, and Mozzarella Salad

⏰ PREP: **5 mins** ◎ COOK: **5 mins** 🍽 SERVES: **6**

Cantaloupe: 1 medium, cut into thin slices or balls
Prosciutto: 8 thin slices
Fresh Mozzarella Cheese: 8 ounces, sliced or torn into pieces
Fresh Basil Leaves: A handful, torn
Balsamic Glaze: 2 tablespoons
Olive Oil: 2 tablespoons

1. Using a sharp knife, peel the cantaloupe and cut it into thin slices. Alternatively, you can scoop it into balls using a melon baller. This will depend on your presentation preference.
2. Arrange the sliced or balled cantaloupe on a large serving platter or distribute it among individual plates.
Drape the slices of prosciutto around and between the melon pieces. Scatter the slices or pieces of fresh mozzarella cheese over the melon and prosciutto.
3. Sprinkle the torn basil leaves over the salad for a fresh, herby touch. Drizzle the olive oil and balsamic glaze over the top. The glaze will add a rich sweetness that complements the prosciutto's saltiness and the melon's freshness.
4. Season lightly with salt and pepper. Be moderate with the salt; the prosciutto adds a significant salty flavor.

Per serving: Calories: 300 kcal, Protein: 15 g, Carbohydrates: 18 g, Fats: 20 g, Fiber: 1 g

Cauliflower Surprise

🕐 PREP: **10 mins** 🎯 COOK: **40 mins** 🍽 SERVES: **4**

Whole Cauliflower: 1 large, leaves removed and stem trimmed
Cream Cheese: 1/2 cup, softened.
Cheddar Cheese: 1/2 cup, grated
Garlic: 2 cloves, minced
Green Onions: 2 tablespoons, finely chopped
Smoked Paprika: 1 teaspoon

1. Preheat your oven to 400°F (200°C). Trim the cauliflower stem so it sits flat, and carefully cut out the core, leaving the head intact.
2. Combine the softened cream cheese, grated cheddar, minced garlic, and green onions in a mixing bowl. Season with smoked paprika, salt, and pepper. Mix until all ingredients are well blended.
3. Gently separate the cauliflower florets at the top just enough to push the cheese mixture inside.
4. Place the stuffed cauliflower on a baking sheet. Drizzle with olive oil and season lightly with salt and pepper. Cover the cauliflower with aluminum foil to prevent the top from burning.
5. Roast in the preheated oven for about 30 minutes. Remove the foil, and continue roasting for another 10 minutes until the outside is golden brown and the cauliflower is tender.

Per serving: Calories: Approximately 220 kcal, Protein: 8 g, Carbohydrates: 10 g, Fats: 17 g, Fiber: 3 g

Broccoli Bruschetta

🕐 PREP: **10 mins** 🎯 COOK: **10 mins** 🍽 SERVES: **6**

French Baguette: 1, sliced into 1/2-inch thick rounds
Broccoli: 1 head, finely chopped
Garlic: 2 cloves, minced
Olive Oil: 2 tablespoons, plus extra for brushing
Parmesan Cheese: 1/4 cup, grated
Salt and Pepper: To taste

1. Wash the broccoli head and chop it into tiny florets, almost to a fine mince. This will help it cook quickly and evenly.
2. Preheat your oven or toaster oven to 400°F (200°C).
3. Brush each baguette slice lightly with olive oil and place on a baking sheet.
Toast in the oven for about 5 minutes or until golden and crisp. Remove and set aside.
4. While the bread is toasting, heat two tablespoons of olive oil in a large skillet over medium heat. Add the minced garlic to the skillet and sauté for about 1 minute until fragrant. Add the finely chopped broccoli, season with salt and pepper, and sauté for about 3-4 minutes, or until the broccoli is tender and bright green.
5. Spoon the cooked broccoli mixture onto each toasted baguette slice. Sprinkle with grated Parmesan cheese while the broccoli is hot so the cheese melts slightly.

Per serving: Calories: 250 kcal, Protein: 9 g, Carbohydrates: 30 g, Fats: 10 g, Fiber: 3 g

Baked Onions with Balsamic Vinegar

⏰ PREP: **10 mins** 🍳 COOK: **25 mins** 🍽️ SERVES: **4**

Large Onions: 4 (such as Vidalia or red onions, peeled)
Balsamic Vinegar: 1/4 cup
Olive Oil: 2 tablespoons
Fresh Thyme: 1 tablespoon or 1 teaspoon of dried thyme
Salt and Pepper: To taste
Butter: 4 small pats (optional, can substitute with more olive oil for vegan version)

1. Preheat your oven to 375°F (190°C).
2. Slice the top of each onion to create a flat surface. Cut a small portion off the bottom so the onion can sit flat, but be careful not to cut into the layers as they need to hold together. Using a knife, make a deep cross in the top of each onion, going about three-quarters of the way down without cutting all the way through.
3. Place the onions in a baking dish. Drizzle each onion with olive oil and balsamic vinegar, ensuring some gets into the cuts. Place a small pat of butter on top of each onion if using. Sprinkle with thyme, salt, and pepper.
4. Cover the dish with aluminum foil and bake in the oven for about 30 minutes. After 30 minutes, remove the foil and continue baking for another 15 minutes or until the onions are tender and the balsamic has caramelized somewhat.

Per serving: Calories: 150 kcal, Protein: 2 g, Carbohydrates: 20 g, Fats: 7 g, Fiber: 3 g, Sodium: Low

Simple Eggplant Mold

⏰ PREP: **20 mins** 🍳 COOK: **40 mins** 🍽️ SERVES: **6**

Eggplant: 2 large, peeled and cubed
Eggs: 2, beaten
Parmesan Cheese: 1/2 cup, grated
Garlic: 2 cloves, minced
Olive Oil: For roasting and greasing
Salt: To taste

1. Preheat your oven to 375°F (190°C).
2. Toss the cubed eggplant with olive oil and salt, then spread on a baking tray. Roast in the oven for about 25-30 minutes or until tender.
3. Once roasted, transfer the eggplant to a food processor. Add the minced garlic, beaten eggs, and grated Parmesan cheese—season with a little more salt to taste. Blend until the mixture is smooth.
4. Grease a mold or small bowls with a bit of olive oil.
Pour the eggplant mixture into the mold, smoothing the top with a spatula.
5. Bake in the oven for about 40 minutes or until the center feels set and the top is slightly golden.
6. Let the mold cool slightly, then carefully invert onto a plate.
For best results, chill the mold in the refrigerator for a few hours to help it set completely before serving.

Per serving: Calories: 180 kcal, Protein: 9 g, Carbohydrates: 13 g, Fats: 11 g, Fiber: 5 g, Sodium: Moderate

Melon Balls in Mayonnaise

⏰ PREP: **10 mins** ⊙ COOK: **10 mins** 🍽 SERVES: **6**

Cantaloupe: 1 medium
Honeydew Melon: 1 medium
Mayonnaise: 1/2 cup
Lemon Juice: 1 tablespoon (to brighten up the mayo)
Mint Leaves: For garnish (optional)

1. Scoop out balls from the cantaloupe and honeydew melon using a melon baller. Ensure that the melon baller rotates smoothly to create perfect balls.
2. Mix the mayonnaise with lemon juice and a pinch of salt in a small bowl. The lemon juice not only thins out the mayonnaise a bit but also adds a light, zesty flavor that complements the sweetness of the melon.
3. Gently mix the melon balls with the mayonnaise dressing. Be careful not to coat them too heavily, as this will overpower their natural flavor.
4. Refrigerate the melon and mayonnaise mixture for about 1 hour to allow the flavors to meld together and the dish to chill thoroughly. Serve chilled, garnished with mint leaves if desired.
5. Variety: This recipe can also be made with watermelon or any other melon variety for a different taste

Per serving: Calories: 200 kcal, Protein: 2 g, Carbohydrates: 20 g, Fats: 13 g, Fiber: 1.5 g, Sodium: moderate

Phyllo Bruschetta Cups

⏰ PREP: **10 mins** ⊙ COOK: **20 mins** 🍽 SERVES: **12**

Phyllo Dough Sheets: 6 sheets, thawed
Prosciutto: 12 thin slices
Ricotta Cheese: 1 cup
Parmesan Cheese: 1/4 cup, grated
Fresh Basil: A few leaves, chopped
Olive Oil: For brushing
1/4 teaspoon ground nutmeg

1. Preheat your oven to 375°F.
2. Carefully unroll the phyllo dough. Cover the sheets with a damp cloth to keep them from drying as you work. Brush a sheet of phyllo with olive oil, then lay another sheet on top. Repeat until you have three layers.
3. Cut the layered phyllo into squares that will fit into mini muffin tin cups. A good size is usually about 4 inches by 4 inches but adjust based on the size of your muffin cups.
4. Press each phyllo square into a muffin cup, gently molding it to form a cup shape. The edges should extend slightly above the rim.
5. Cut each slice of prosciutto to fit inside the phyllo cups and press one into each cup. Mix the ricotta with the grated Parmesan cheese and chopped basil. Spoon this mixture into each phyllo cup, filling them about three-quarters full.
6. Bake in the oven for about 15 minutes or until the phyllo is golden brown and crispy.

Per serving: Calories: 120 kcal, Protein: 6 g, Carbohydrates: 8 g, Fats: 8 g, Fiber: 0.5 g

Savory Ricotta with Pistachiosse

⏰ PREP: **10 mins** 🍳 COOK: **10 mins** 🍽️ SERVES: **4**

Ricotta Cheese: 1 cup, well-drained
Pistachio Nuts: 1/4 cup, shelled and roughly chopped
Olive Oil: 1 tablespoon, extra virgin
Fresh Herbs: Such as chives or basil, finely chopped
Salt and Pepper: To taste

1.If the ricotta is wet, strain it through a fine-mesh sieve to remove excess liquid.
2. Place the ricotta in a mixing bowl and season with salt and pepper.
Stir in olive oil and half of the chopped herbs to incorporate evenly.
3. Transfer the ricotta mixture to a serving bowl or plate.
Sprinkle with chopped pistachios and the remaining herbs.
4. Serve with toasted bread, crackers, or vegetable slices.
Per serving: Calories: 200 kcal, Protein: 10 g, Carbohydrates: 8 g, Fats: 14 g, Fiber: 1 g

Cabbage with Balsamic Vinegar

⏰ PREP: **10 mins** 🍳 COOK: **20 mins** 🍽️ SERVES: **6**

Cabbage: 1 medium head, cored and thinly sliced
Balsamic Vinegar: 3 tablespoons
Olive Oil: 2 tablespoons
Garlic: 2 cloves, minced
Salt and Pepper: To taste
Optional: Red Pepper Flakes: For a spicy kick

1. Rinse the cabbage under cold water. Remove the outer leaves if they are challenging or damaged.
2. Core the cabbage and slice it thinly. This will help it cook evenly and absorb more flavor.
3. Heat the olive oil in a large skillet over medium heat.
Add the minced garlic to the skillet and sauté for about 1 minute or until fragrant. Be careful not to let it burn.
4. Add the sliced cabbage to the skillet. Stir well to coat the cabbage with oil and garlic.
Continue cooking the cabbage, stirring occasionally, for about 15 minutes or until it is tender and some edges begin caramelizing.
5. Pour the balsamic vinegar over the cabbage in the skillet. Stir well to distribute the vinegar evenly.
Season with salt, pepper, and red pepper flakes if using. Cook for 5 minutes, allowing the vinegar to reduce slightly and the flavors to meld together.
Per serving: Calories: 90 kcal, Protein: 2 g, Carbohydrates: 10 g, Fats: 5 g, Fiber: 3 g, Sodium: Low

Glazed Onions

⏰ PREP: **5 mins** ◎ COOK: **25 mins** 🍽 SERVES: **4**

Onions: 4 large onions, peeled and sliced into rings
Butter: 2 tablespoons
Brown Sugar: 2 tablespoons
Balsamic Vinegar: 2 tablespoons
Salt: 1/4 teaspoon, or to taste
Black Pepper: 1/4 teaspoon, or to taste

1. Melt the butter in a large skillet over medium heat. Ensure the skillet is large enough to accommodate the onions without overcrowding, as this will help them caramelize rather than steam.
2. Add the sliced onions to the skillet, stirring to coat them with the melted butter.
3. Cook the onions, stirring occasionally, for about 10-15 minutes or until they soften and turn translucent.
4. Sprinkle the brown sugar over the onions and add the balsamic vinegar.
5. Reduce the heat to medium-low and continue cooking for another 10-15 minutes, stirring frequently. The onions should begin to caramelize and turn a deep golden brown. The vinegar and sugar will reduce and form a thick, rich glaze.
6. Season with salt and pepper towards the end of cooking. Adjust according to your taste preferences.

Per serving: Calories: 150 kcal, Protein: 1 g, Carbohydrates: 20 g, Fats: 7 g, Fiber: 2 g, Sodium: 150

Celery and Walnuts in Saffron Aspic

⏰ PREP: **20 mins** ◎ COOK: **10 mins** 🍽 SERVES: **6**

Unflavored Gelatin: 2 tablespoons (about two packets)
Chicken or Vegetable Broth: 2 cups
Saffron Threads: A pinch
Lemon Juice: 2 tablespoons
Celery: 2 cups, finely chopped
Walnuts: 1 cup, roughly chopped

1. In a small bowl, sprinkle gelatin over 1/2 cup of cold water to let it bloom (soften) for about 5 minutes.
2. In a saucepan, heat the broth over medium heat. Add the saffron threads, allowing them to steep as the broth warms.
3. Once the broth is hot but not boiling, add the bloomed gelatin and whisk until the gelatin is completely dissolved.
Remove from heat and stir in the lemon juice. Season with salt and pepper to taste. Let the mixture cool to room temperature.
4. Lightly oil a mold or individual molds with a neutral oil to help unmold them later. Place a layer of chopped celery and walnuts at the bottom of the mold.
5. Pour the cooled gelatin mixture over the celery and walnuts until the mold is filled.
6. Refrigerate the aspic for at least 4-6 hours or until firmly set.
7. To unmold, briefly dip the bottom of the mold in warm water and then invert it onto a serving plate.

Per serving: Calories: 150 kcal, Protein: 4 g, Carbohydrates: 8 g, Fats: 10 g, Fiber: 2 g, Sodium: Low

Greek Country Salad (Horiatiki)

⏰ PREP: **10 mins** 🔍 COOK: **10 mins** 🍽️ SERVES: **4**

Tomatoes: 3 large, ripe, cut into wedges
Cucumbers: 1 large, peeled and sliced into thick half-moons
Red Onion: 1 small, thinly sliced
Kalamata Olives: 1/2 cup
Feta Cheese: 200 grams, sliced or crumbled
Extra Virgin Olive Oil: 3 tablespoons

1. Wash the tomatoes and cucumbers. Cut the tomatoes into wedges and the cucumbers into thick half-moons. Peel and thinly slice the red onion.
2. Combine the tomato wedges, cucumber, and red onion slices in a large salad bowl. Add the Kalamata olives to the bowl.
3. Top the salad with a thick slice of feta cheese or crumble the feta over the vegetables. Drizzle the extra virgin olive oil over the entire salad.
4. Gently toss the salad before serving to distribute the olive oil evenly.
Per serving: Calories: 250 kcal, Protein: 7 g, Carbohydrates: 10 g, Fats: 20 g, Fiber: 2 g, Sodium: Low

Green Pea Soup

⏰ PREP: **10 mins** 🔍 COOK: **20 mins** 🍽️ SERVES: **4**

Green Peas: 4 cups (fresh or frozen)
Onion: 1 medium, chopped
Vegetable Broth: 4 cups
Mint Leaves: A handful, plus extra for garnish
Salt and Pepper: To taste
Olive Oil: 2 tablespoons

1. In a large pot, heat the olive oil over medium heat. Add the chopped onion and sauté until it becomes translucent and slightly golden, about 5 minutes.
2. Add the green peas to the pot (if using frozen, there's no need to thaw them first). Pour in the vegetable broth and bring the mixture to a boil.
3. Reduce heat and simmer for 10 minutes or until the peas are tender.
4. Add the fresh mint leaves to the pot.
5. An immersion blender will puree the soup directly in the pot until smooth. Alternatively, carefully transfer the soup to a blender and puree it in batches.
6. Return the soup to the pot if using a standard blender. Heat it through if necessary.
7. Season with salt and pepper to taste. Adjust the consistency by adding more broth or water if it's too thick.
Per serving: Calories: 200 kcal, Protein: 8 g, Carbohydrates: 30 g, Fats: 5 g, Fiber: 8 g, Sodium: Low

Cream of Cucumber Soup

⏰ PREP: **10 mins** 🔍 COOK: **10 mins** 🍽 SERVES: **4**

Cucumbers: 2 large, peeled, seeded, and chopped
Onion: 1 medium, chopped
Garlic: 2 cloves, minced
Chicken or Vegetable Broth: 3 cups
Heavy Cream: 1 cup
Fresh Dill: 2 tablespoons, chopped, plus extra for garnish
Lemon Juice: 1 tablespoon
Olive Oil: 1 tablespoon

1. In a large pot, heat the olive oil over medium heat.
2. Add the chopped onion and minced garlic, sautéing until the onion is translucent and soft, about 5 minutes.
3. Add the chopped cucumbers to the pot and cook for another 5 minutes.
4. Pour in the chicken or vegetable broth and bring the mixture to a simmer.
5. Remove the pot from the heat. Stir in the chopped fresh dill.
6. Using an immersion blender, puree the soup in the pot until smooth. Alternatively, carefully transfer the soup to a blender or food processor.
7. If serving warm, return the blended soup to the pot, stir in the cream, and warm it over low heat, just until heated through. Do not let it boil after adding the cream. If serving chilled, transfer the soup to a mixing bowl, stir in the cream, and then refrigerate for at least 2 hours until cold.

Per serving: Calories: 200 kcal, Protein: 3 g, Carbohydrates: 12 g, Fats: 15 g, Fiber: 2 g, Sodium: Low

Muhammara Salad

⏰ PREP: **10 mins** 🔍 COOK: **10 mins** 🍽 SERVES: **4**

Roasted Red Peppers: 2 large, peeled and chopped
Walnuts: 1/2 cup, toasted and roughly chopped
Garlic: 1 clove, minced
Lemon Juice: 1 tablespoon
Pomegranate Molasses: 1 tablespoon
Mixed Greens: 4 cups (such as arugula or baby spinach)

1. Combine the roasted red peppers, walnuts, minced garlic, lemon juice, and pomegranate molasses in a food processor. Blend until the mixture reaches a smooth yet slightly chunky consistency, ensuring it has enough body to coat the greens.
2. Place the mixed greens in a large bowl. Pour the Muhammara mixture over the greens. Using tongs or salad servers, gently toss the greens until they are evenly coated with the dressing.
3. Transfer the salad to serving plates or a large platter. The Muhammara not only dresses the greens but also imparts a vibrant, slightly tangy flavor profile, enhanced by the sweetness of pomegranate and the nuttiness of walnuts.

Per serving: Calories: 150 kcal, Protein: 3 g, Carbohydrates: 8 g, Fats: 12 g, Fiber: 2 g, Sodium: Low

No-Pasta Zucchini Noodle Salad

⏰ PREP: **20 mins** ◎ COOK: **20 mins** 🍽 SERVES: **4**

Zucchini: 4 large, spiralized
Cherry Tomatoes: 1 cup, halved
Red Onion: 1 small, thinly sliced
Black Olives: 1/2 cup, pitted and halved
Feta Cheese: 1/2 cup, crumbled
Fresh Basil: A handful, chopped
Olive Oil: 3 tablespoons
Lemon Juice: 2 tablespoons

1. Use a spiralizer to turn the zucchini into noodles. If you don't have a spiralizer, a vegetable peeler can create long, thin strips.
2. Place the zucchini noodles in a colander, sprinkle with a bit of salt, and let them sit for about 10 minutes to release excess water. Gently pat dry with paper towels.
3. Combine the drained zucchini noodles, halved cherry tomatoes, thinly sliced red onion, black olives, and crumbled feta cheese in a large bowl.
4. Whisk together the olive oil and lemon juice in a small bowl or jar—season with salt and pepper to taste.
5. Pour the dressing over the salad ingredients and gently toss to coat everything evenly.

Per serving: Calories: 180 kcal, Protein: 5 g, Carbohydrates: 10 g, Fats: 14 g, Fiber: 2 g, Sodium: Low

Radicchio and Ricotta Linguine Salad

⏰ PREP: **15 mins** ◎ COOK: **15 mins** 🍽 SERVES: **4**

Linguine: 12 ounces (about 340 grams)
Radicchio: 1 head, thinly sliced
Ricotta Cheese: 1 cup
Garlic: 2 cloves, minced
Olive Oil: 3 tablespoons
Parmesan Cheese: 1/2 cup, freshly grated

1. Bring a large pot of salted water to a boil. Cook the linguine according to package instructions until al dente.
2. Reserve 1 cup of pasta water, drain the pasta and set aside.
3. While the pasta cooks, heat the olive oil in a large skillet over medium heat. Add the minced garlic and sauté for about 1 minute until fragrant. Add the sliced radicchio to the skillet. Cook, stirring frequently, until wilted and tender, about 5-7 minutes.
4. Season with salt, pepper, and optional red pepper flakes.
5. Reduce the heat to low and add the cooked linguine to the skillet with the radicchio. Add the ricotta cheese and half of the reserved pasta water. Toss gently to combine, adding more pasta water if needed to create a creamy sauce. Cook for 2-3 minutes until everything is heated and the sauce coats the pasta evenly.

Per serving: Calories: 480 kcal, Protein: 19 g, Carbohydrates: 65 g, Fats: 18 g, Fiber: 4 g, Sodium: Low

Cobb Salad with Roasted Chickpeas & Creamy Tahini

⏰ PREP: **20 mins** 🔍 COOK: **25 mins** 🍽️ SERVES: **4**

Chickpeas: 1 can (15 ounces), drained, rinsed, and dried
Mixed Greens: 6 cups (such as spinach and arugula)
Avocado: 1 large, diced
Tahini: 3 tablespoons
Lemon Juice: 2 tablespoons
Salt and Pepper: To taste

1. Preheat the oven to 400°F (200°C).
2. Toss the chickpeas with olive oil (if available within your ingredient limit) and a pinch of salt and pepper. Spread them on a baking sheet.
3. Roast for 20-25 minutes, shaking the pan halfway through, until they are crispy and golden. Let them cool.
4. In a small bowl, whisk together the tahini and lemon juice. Add a little water if needed to reach a pourable consistency, and season with salt and pepper.
5. In a large salad bowl, toss the mixed greens and diced avocado. Add the roasted chickpeas.

Per serving: Calories: 300 kcal, Protein: 9 g, Carbohydrates: 30 g, Fats: 18 g, Fiber: 8 g, Sodium: Low

Crepes in Vegetable Broth Soup

⏰ PREP: **10 mins** 🔍 COOK: **15 mins** 🍽️ SERVES: **4**

For the Crepes:
All-Purpose Flour: 1/2 cup
Eggs: 2
Milk: 3/4 cup
For the Soup:
Vegetable Broth: 6 cups
Salt and Pepper: To taste

1. Whisk together the flour, eggs, and milk in a mixing bowl until the batter is smooth. Let the batter rest for about 5 minutes to ensure it thickens slightly for easier handling.
2. Heat a lightly oiled, non-stick skillet over medium heat. Pour or scoop the batter onto the skillet, using approximately 1/4 cup for each crepe. Tilt the pan in a circular motion so the batter coats the surface evenly.
3. Roast each crepe for about 2 minutes until the bottom is light brown. Loosen with a spatula, turn, and cook the other side. Set aside.
4. Bring the vegetable broth to a simmer in a large pot—season with salt and pepper to taste.
5. Roll the crepes and slice them into thin ribbons. Place the sliced crepe ribbons into serving bowls.

Per serving: Calories: 150 kcal, Protein: 6 g, Carbohydrates: 20 g, Fats: 5 g, Fiber: 0 g, Sodium: Low

Cream of Cauliflower & Millet Soup

🕐 PREP: **10 mins** 🔍 COOK: **25 mins** 🍽 SERVES: **4**

Cauliflower: 1 large head, chopped
Millet: 1/2 cup, rinsed
Vegetable Broth: 4 cups
Onion: 1 medium, chopped
Garlic: 2 cloves, minced
Olive Oil: 2 tablespoons

1. In a large pot, heat the olive oil over medium heat.
2. Add the chopped onion and minced garlic, sautéing until the onion becomes translucent and softens, about 3-5 minutes.
3. Add the chopped cauliflower and rinsed millet to the pot. Stir to combine with the aromatics.
4. Pour in the vegetable broth. Bring the mixture to a boil, then reduce the heat and simmer covered for about 20 minutes, or until the cauliflower and millet are both tender.
5. Once the vegetables and millet are cooked, use an immersion blender to puree the soup directly in the pot until smooth. If you don't have an immersion blender, carefully transfer the soup to a standard blender in batches and blend until smooth. Add more vegetable broth or water to reach your desired consistency if the soup is too thick.

Per serving: Calories: 200 kcal, Protein: 6 g, Carbohydrates: 30 g, Fats: 7 g, Fiber: 5 g, Sodium: Low

Rice & Parsley Soup

🕐 PREP: **10 mins** 🔍 COOK: **25 mins** 🍽 SERVES: **4**

Rice: 1/2 cup long-grain or short-grain white rice
Fresh Parsley: 1 cup, finely chopped
Vegetable Broth: 6 cups
Onion: 1 medium, finely chopped
Olive Oil: 2 tablespoons
Salt: To taste

1. In a large pot, heat the olive oil over medium heat. Add the chopped onion and sauté until translucent and soft, about 5 minutes.
2. Add the rice to the pot and stir to coat it with the olive oil and onion. Pour in the vegetable broth and bring the mixture to a boil.
3. Reduce the heat to low and let the soup simmer for about 20 minutes or until the rice is tender.
4. Stir in the finely chopped parsley and season with salt to taste. Let the soup simmer for 5 minutes to let the flavors meld together.
5. Taste and adjust seasoning if necessary. Ladle the soup into bowls and serve hot.

Per serving: Calories: 180 kcal, Protein: 4 g, Carbohydrates: 30 g, Fats: 5 g, Fiber: 1 g, Sodium: Low

Pasta with Chickpea Soup

🕐 PREP: **10 mins** 🔍 COOK: **25 mins** 🍽️ SERVES: **4**

Chickpeas: 1 can (15 ounces), drained and rinsed
Small Pasta: 1 cup (such as ditalini, orzo, or small shells)
Vegetable Broth: 6 cups
Garlic: 2 cloves, minced
Olive Oil: 2 tablespoons
Salt and Pepper: To taste

1. In a large pot, heat the olive oil over medium heat. Add the minced garlic and sauté for about 1-2 minutes, until fragrant but not browned.
2. Add the drained and rinsed chickpeas to the pot and stir to coat them with the garlic and oil.
3. Pour in the vegetable broth and bring the mixture to a boil.
4. Add the pasta to the boiling broth and cook according to the package instructions, usually about 8-10 minutes, until al dente.
5. Once the pasta is cooked, reduce the heat to a simmer. Season with salt and pepper to taste. Adjust the soup's consistency by adding water if it's too thick or letting it simmer a bit longer if it's too thin.
6. Ladle the soup into bowls, ensuring reasonable amounts of chickpeas and pasta are in each serving.

Per serving: Calories: 300 kcal, Protein: 10 g, Carbohydrates: 45 g, Fats: 8 g, Fiber: 6 g, Sodium: Low

Creamy Broccoli Soup

🕐 PREP: **10 mins** 🔍 COOK: **20 mins** 🍽️ SERVES: **4**

Broccoli: 4 cups, chopped into florets
Onion: 1 medium, chopped
Garlic: 2 cloves, minced
Chicken or Vegetable Broth: 4 cups
Heavy Cream: 1 cup
Olive Oil: 1 tablespoon

1. In a large pot, heat the olive oil over medium heat.
2. Add the chopped onion and minced garlic. Sauté until the onion is translucent and fragrant, about 3-5 minutes.
3. Add the broccoli florets to the pot and stir to mix with the aromatics. Pour in the chicken or vegetable broth, ensuring the broccoli is completely submerged.
4. Bring to a boil, reduce the heat, and simmer until the broccoli is tender, about 10-15 minutes.
5. An immersion blender will puree the soup directly in the pot until smooth. If using a standard blender, carefully transfer the soup in batches and blend until soft, then return to the pot.
6. Stir in the heavy cream and warm the soup, but do not allow it to boil. Season with salt and pepper to taste.

Per serving: Calories: 250 kcal, Protein: 6 g, Carbohydrates: 15 g, Fats: 19 g, Fiber: 3 g, Sodium: Low

Vegan Nicoise Salad

⏰ PREP: **15 mins** ◉ COOK: **15 mins** 🍽 SERVES: **4**

Baby Potatoes: 8-10, boiled and halved
Green Beans: 1 cup, blanched
Cherry Tomatoes: 1 cup, halved
Chickpeas: 1 cup, cooked or canned and drained
Mixed Salad Greens: 4 cups
Olive Oil and Lemon Juice Dressing: 1/4 cup olive oil mixed with two tablespoons lemon juice, salt, and pepper to taste

1. Boil the baby potatoes until tender, about 10-15 minutes, then halve them.
Blanch the green beans in boiling water for 4 minutes, then cool them in ice water to retain their color and crispness.
2. Whisk together the olive oil, lemon juice, salt, and pepper in a small bowl. Adjust the seasoning according to your taste.
3. In a large salad bowl, layer the mixed salad greens.
Arrange the boiled potatoes, blanched green beans, cherry tomatoes, and chickpeas on top of the greens.
4. Drizzle the olive oil and lemon juice dressing over the salad.
5. Toss gently to combine all the ingredients right before serving.
Per serving: Calories: 300 kcal, Protein: 8 g, Carbohydrates: 40 g, Fats: 12 g, Fiber: 8 g, Sodium: Low

Aubergine Crete Salad

⏰ PREP: **10 mins** ◉ COOK: **25 mins** 🍽 SERVES: **4**

Aubergines (Eggplants): 2 large, cut into cubes
Tomatoes: 2 large, diced
Feta Cheese: 1/2 cup, crumbled
Olive Oil: 3 tablespoons
Fresh Parsley: A handful, chopped
Lemon Juice: 2 tablespoons (or to taste)

1. Preheat your oven to 400°F (200°C).
2. Toss the cubed aubergines with two tablespoons of olive oil and spread them on a baking sheet in a single layer.
3. Roast in the oven for about 20-25 minutes, turning halfway through, until the aubergines are tender and golden brown.
4. Combine the roasted aubergines, diced tomatoes, and crumbled feta cheese in a large bowl.
5. Whisk together the remaining tablespoon of olive oil and lemon juice in a small bowl. Pour this dressing over the salad.
6. Sprinkle chopped parsley over the salad and toss everything together gently to mix.
Serve the salad warm or at room temperature.
Per serving: Calories: 220 kcal, Protein: 5 g, Carbohydrates: 15 g, Fats: 16 g, Fiber: 5 g, Sodium: Low

Taramosalata Salad

⏰ PREP: **10 mins** 🍳 COOK: **10 mins** 🍽️ SERVES: **4**

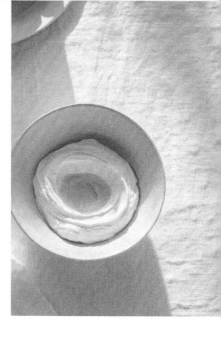

Tarama (Carp or Cod Roe): 100 grams
Day-Old White Bread: 100 grams (crusts removed, if preferred)
Olive Oil: 1 cup
Lemon Juice: From 1-2 lemons (to taste)
Onion: 1 small, grated (optional for added flavor)
Garlic: 1 clove, minced (optional)

1. Soak the bread in water for a few minutes until soft. Squeeze out the excess water thoroughly. This step is crucial to avoid a watery dip.
2. Combine the soaked bread, tarama, optional onion, and garlic in a food processor. Pulse to mix.
3. While the processor is running, slowly drizzle in the olive oil, allowing it to emulsify with the tarama and bread mixture.
4. Add lemon juice gradually, tasting as you go, until the desired acidity is reached. The lemon juice adds flavor and helps balance the richness of the olive oil and roe.
5. Add a little water or more lemon juice to adjust the consistency if the taramosalata is too thick.
Taste and adjust the seasoning, adding more lemon juice if needed. Remember that trauma is already salty, so additional salt is usually unnecessary.

Per serving: Calories: 300 kcal, Protein: 5 g, Carbohydrates: 5 g, Fats: 30 g, Fiber: 0 g, Sodium: Low

Sautéed Broccoli Rabe Salad

⏰ PREP: **10 mins** 🍳 COOK: **10 mins** 🍽️ SERVES: **4**

Broccoli Rabe: 1 bunch (about 1 pound), trimmed and washed
Garlic: 3 cloves, thinly sliced
Olive Oil: 2 tablespoons
Red Pepper Flakes: A pinch (optional for a bit of heat)
Salt: To taste
Lemon Juice: From 1 lemon (optional, for finishing)

1. Bring a large pot of salted water to a boil.
2. Add the broccoli rabe and blanch for 1-2 minutes to soften slightly and reduce bitterness.
3. Drain in a colander and rinse under cold water to stop cooking. Squeeze out excess water.
4. Heat the olive oil in a large skillet over medium heat.
Add the garlic and red pepper flakes, sautéing until the garlic is fragrant but not browned, about 1 minute.
5. Add the blanched broccoli rabe to the skillet. Toss to coat with the olive oil and garlic. Sauté for about 5-7 minutes until the broccoli rabe is tender but slightly crisp.

Per serving: Calories: 80 kcal, Protein: 4 g, Carbohydrates: 4 g, Fats: 6 g, Fiber: 3 g, Sodium: Low

Arugula with Fennel & Balsamic Salad

⏰ PREP: **10 mins** 🍳 COOK: **10 mins** 🍽️ SERVES: **4**

Arugula: 4 cups (fresh, baby arugula)
Fennel Bulb: 1 medium, thinly sliced
Balsamic Vinegar: 2 tablespoons
Olive Oil: 3 tablespoons
Salt: To taste
Pepper: To taste

1. Trim the fennel bulb by cutting off the stalks and removing the tough outer layer. Slice the bulb thinly, either by hand or with a mandoline, to get nice, even slices.
2. In a large salad bowl, combine the arugula and sliced fennel.
3. Whisk together the balsamic vinegar and olive oil in a small bowl—season with salt and pepper to taste.
4. Drizzle the balsamic dressing over the arugula and fennel. Toss gently to coat the salad evenly.
5. Serve immediately for the freshest flavor, as arugula wilts quickly once dressed.

Per serving: Calories: 120 kcal, Protein: 1 g, Carbohydrates: 5 g, Fats: 11 g, Fiber: 2 g, Sodium: Low

Baked "Unstuffed" Tomatoes Chopped Salad

⏰ PREP: **10 mins** 🍳 COOK: **15 mins** 🍽️ SERVES: **4**

Large Tomatoes: 4, tops sliced off and insides carefully hollowed out
Italian Salad Mix: 2 cups, chopped (including ingredients like cucumbers, red onions, bell peppers, and olives)
Mozzarella Cheese: 1/2 cup, diced or shredded
Italian Dressing: 1/4 cup, ready-made or homemade
Fresh Basil: A few leaves, chopped for garnish

1. Preheat your oven to 375°F (190°C).
2. Slice the tops off the tomatoes and hollow out the insides with a spoon. Be careful to preserve the integrity of the walls.
3. Lightly salt the inside of each tomato and place them upside down on a paper towel for a few minutes to drain any excess moisture.
4. Combine the chopped Italian salad mix with Italian dressing in a mixing bowl. Mix well to ensure everything is evenly coated. Adjust the seasoning with salt and pepper.
5. Spoon the salad mix into each hollowed-out tomato until nearly complete. Top each with either diced or shredded mozzarella cheese, according to your preference.
6. Place the stuffed tomatoes on a baking tray.
7. Bake in the preheated oven for about 15-20 minutes, or until the tomatoes are tender and the cheese is melted and slightly golden.

Per serving: Calories: 150 kcal, Protein: 6 g, Carbohydrates: 8 g, Fats: 10 g, Fiber: 2 g, Sodium: Low

Grilled Peach & Burrata Salad

⏰ PREP: **10 mins** ⏱ COOK: **10 mins** 🍽 SERVES: **4**

Peaches: 4 medium, halved and pitted
Burrata Cheese: 8 ounces
Arugula: 4 cups, washed and dried
Balsamic Glaze: 2 tablespoons
Olive Oil: 2 tablespoons, plus extra for brushing peaches
Fresh Basil: A few leaves for garnish
Salt and Pepper: To taste

1. Heat the grill or a grill pan to medium heat.
2. Brush the cut sides of the peaches with olive oil to prevent sticking.
3. Place the peaches cut-side down on the grill and cook for about 4-5 minutes or until they have excellent grill marks and start to soften. Turn them over and grill for another 2-3 minutes. Remove from the grill and let them cool slightly before slicing.
4. Toss the arugula with 2 tablespoons of olive oil in a large salad bowl and season with salt and pepper.
5. Arrange the arugula on serving plates.
6. Slice the grilled peaches and arrange them over the arugula. Place pieces of burrata cheese around the peaches.

Per serving: Calories: 290 kcal, Protein: 10 g, Carbohydrates: 20 g, Fats: 20 g, Fiber: 3 g, Sodium:

Fregola with Herbs & Pine Nuts Salad

⏰ PREP: **10 mins** ⏱ COOK: **10 mins** 🍽 SERVES: **6**

Fregola: 1 cup (toasted if available, otherwise regular)
Parsley: 1/2 cup, chopped
Mint: 1/4 cup, chopped
Pine Nuts: 1/4 cup, toasted
Lemon Zest: From 1 lemon
Lemon Juice: 2 tablespoons
Olive Oil: 3 tablespoons

1. Bring a large pot of salted water to a boil. Add the fregola and cook according to the package instructions until al dente, usually around 10-15 minutes.
2. Drain and rinse under cold water to stop the cooking process and cool it down. Set aside.
3. In a dry skillet, toast the pine nuts over medium heat, shaking the pan frequently until golden and fragrant. This usually takes about 3-4 minutes. Watch them closely to avoid burning.
4. Whisk together the lemon juice, olive oil, salt, and pepper in a small bowl.
5. Combine the cooked fregola, chopped parsley, chopped mint, toasted pine nuts, and lemon zest in a large salad bowl.
Pour the dressing over the salad and toss well to combine all the ingredients.

Per serving: Calories: 300 kcal, Protein: 6 g, Carbohydrates: 35 g, Fats: 15 g, Fiber: 4 g, Sodium: Low

Pumpkin & Bean Soup

⏰ PREP: **15 mins** ◉ COOK: **30 mins** 🍽 SERVES: **4**

Pumpkin: 2 cups, peeled and cubed (or canned pureed pumpkin for a quicker option)
White Beans: 1 can (15 ounces), drained and rinsed
Vegetable Broth: 4 cups
Onion: 1 medium, diced
Garlic: 2 cloves, minced
Olive Oil: 2 tablespoons

1. Heat the olive oil in a large pot over medium heat.
2. Add the diced onion and minced garlic, sautéing until the onion becomes translucent and softens for about 5 minutes.
3. Add cubed pumpkin to the pot and cook for a few minutes.
4. Pour in the vegetable broth, bring the mixture to a boil, then reduce heat and simmer until the pumpkin is tender, about 20 minutes.
5. Stir in the white beans and continue simulating for another 10 minutes, allowing the flavors to meld.
6. Using a cubed pumpkin, use an immersion blender to puree the soup in the pot until smooth. Using canned pumpkin, you can stir well to combine as the texture should already be pretty smooth.

Per serving: Calories: 250 kcal, Protein: 8 g, Carbohydrates: 35 g, Fats: 8 g, Fiber: 9 g, Sodium: Low

Cream of Cannellini Bean Soup with Sage & Lemon

⏰ PREP: **10 mins** ◉ COOK: **20 mins** 🍽 SERVES: **4**

Cannellini Beans: 2 cans (15 ounces each), drained and rinsed
Vegetable Broth: 4 cups
Fresh Sage: 8 leaves, plus extra for garnish
Lemon: 1, zest and juice
Garlic: 2 cloves, minced
Olive Oil: 2 tablespoons

1. In a large pot, heat the olive oil over medium heat.
2. Add the minced garlic and sage leaves. Sauté until the garlic is fragrant and slightly golden, about 1-2 minutes.
3. Add the cannellini beans to the pot and stir to combine with the garlic and sage.
4. Pour in the vegetable broth and bring the mixture to a simmer. Let it cook for about 15 minutes, allowing the flavors to meld together.
5. Remove the pot from the heat. Use an immersion blender to puree the soup directly in the pot until smooth and creamy. If using a standard blender, carefully transfer the soup in batches and blend until soft, then return to the pot.
6. Stir in the lemon zest and juice, adjusting the amount to taste—season with salt and pepper.

Per serving: Calories: 250 kcal, Protein: 10 g, Carbohydrates: 35 g, Fats: 8 g, Fiber: 8 g, Sodium: Low

Tomato Soup with Parmesan Crostini

⏰ PREP: **10 mins** ◎ COOK: **20 mins** 🍽 SERVES: **2 -4**

Canned Tomatoes: 2 cans (28 ounces each), crushed or dice
Vegetable Broth: 3 cups
Garlic: 2 cloves, minced
Baguette: 1, sliced into rounds
Parmesan Cheese: As needed, grated
Olive Oil: For drizzling and cooking

1. Heat a drizzle of olive oil over medium heat in a large pot.
2. Add the minced garlic and sauté until fragrant, about 1 minute.
3. Pour in the canned tomatoes and vegetable broth. Bring to a boil, reduce heat, and simmer for 15-20 minutes.
4. Preheat the oven to 375°F (190°C).
5. Place baguette slices on a baking sheet. Drizzle with olive oil and sprinkle generously with grated Parmesan cheese.
6. Bake until the crostini are golden, and the cheese is melted about 10 mins.
7. An immersion blender will puree the soup directly in the pot until smooth. If using a standard blender, carefully transfer the soup in batches and blend until soft.
8. Taste the soup and adjust the seasoning with salt and pepper if necessary.

Per serving: Calories: 300 kcal, Protein: 8 g, Carbohydrates: 35 g, Fats: 15 g, Fiber: 5 g, Sodium: Low

Onion & Mushroom Soup

⏰ PREP: **15 mins** ◎ COOK: **30 mins** 🍽 SERVES: **4**

Onions: 3 large, thinly sliced
Mushrooms: 2 cups, sliced (any variety like button or cremini)
Vegetable Broth: 4 cups
Garlic: 2 cloves, minced
Butter: 2 tablespoons (or olive oil for a vegan option)
Salt and Pepper: To taste

1. Melt the butter in a large pot over medium heat. Add the thinly sliced onions and minced garlic, cooking until the onions become soft and translucent, about 5-7 minutes.
2. Increase the heat to medium-high and add the sliced mushrooms. Cook until the mushrooms have released their moisture and the onions and mushrooms are beginning to caramelize, about 10-15 minutes. Stir frequently to prevent sticking and ensure even cooking.
3. Once the onions and mushrooms are cooked and browned, add the vegetable broth. Bring the mixture to a simmer.
Add dried thyme if using, and season with salt and pepper to taste.
4. Reduce heat and let the soup simmer gently for about 20 minutes, allowing the flavors to meld together.

Per serving: Calories: 150 kcal, Protein: 4 g, Carbohydrates: 15 g, Fats: 8 g, Fiber: 2 g, Sodium: Low

Multicolor Conchiglie Salad

⏰ PREP: **10 mins** 🔍 COOK: **10 mins** 🍽 SERVES: **4**

Conchiglie Pasta: 2 cups, uncooked
Cherry Tomatoes: 1 cup, mixed colors, halved.
Arugula: 1 cup
Parmesan Cheese: 1/2 cup, shaved
Olive Oil: 2 tablespoons
Salt and Pepper: To taste

1. Bring a pot of salted water to a boil. Add the conchiglie pasta and cook according to the package directions until al dente.
2. Drain the pasta and rinse under cold water to cool. Set aside.
3. Combine the cooked and cooled pasta, halved cherry tomatoes, and fresh arugula in a large mixing bowl.
4. Drizzle with olive oil, and season with salt and pepper to taste. Toss well to mix the ingredients.
5. Just before serving, sprinkle the shaved Parmesan cheese over the top of the salad.
6. Toss lightly once more to distribute the cheese throughout the salad.

Per serving: Calories: 300 kcal, Protein: 10 g, Carbohydrates: 40 g, Fats: 12 g, Fiber: 2 g, Sodium: Low

Tomato & White Bean Soup

⏰ PREP: **10 mins** 🔍 COOK: **20 mins** 🍽 SERVES: **4**

Canned Tomatoes: 2 cans (28 ounces each), crushed
White Beans: 1 can (15 ounces), drained and rinsed
Vegetable Broth: 4 cups
Garlic: 2 cloves, minced
Olive Oil: 2 tablespoons
Salt and Pepper: To taste

1. In a large pot, heat the olive oil over medium heat.
2. Add the minced garlic and sauté until fragrant, about 1-2 minutes.
3. Add the crushed tomatoes and vegetable broth to the pot. Stir to combine.
4. Bring the mixture to a boil, then reduce the heat and let it simmer for about 10 minutes to melt the flavors.
5. Stir in the white beans and continue to simmer the soup for another 10 minutes, allowing the beans to warm through and the flavors to integrate further.
6. Blend (Optional):Use an immersion blender to partially or fully blend the soup in the pot for a smoother texture. Alternatively, carefully mix the soup in batches with a standard blender, then return it to the pot.
7. Season the soup with salt and pepper to taste.
8. Serve hot, with crusty bread if desired, or a sprinkle of Parmesan cheese or fresh herbs.

Per serving: Calories: 220 kcal, Protein: 8 g, Carbohydrates: 33 g, Fats: 6 g, Fiber: 8 g, Sodium: Low

PROTEINS

Chicken Donair Plate

🕙 PREP: **15 mins** 🔍 COOK: **10 mins** 🍽 SERVES: **4**

Chicken Thighs: 1 pound, thinly sliced or chopped
Donair Spice Mix: 1 tablespoon (a blend typically including garlic powder, onion powder, paprika, and a pinch of cayenne)
Pita Bread: 4 rounds
Tomatoes: 2 large, diced
Onion: 1 large, thinly sliced
Tzatziki Sauce: 1 cup (can be store-bought or homemade with Greek yogurt, cucumber, garlic, and lemon juice)

1. Toss the chicken thighs with the donair spice mix in a mixing bowl until well-coated.
2. Heat a skillet over medium-high heat and add the chicken. Cook for 5-7 minutes, stirring occasionally, until the chicken is fully cooked and slightly crispy on the edges.
3. While the chicken cooks, dice the tomatoes and thinly slice the onion.
4. Wrap the pita bread in foil and warm it in the oven at 350°F for about 5 minutes, or quickly warm it in a dry skillet over medium heat for about 30 seconds per side.
5. Serve each donair plate with a side of tzatziki sauce to drizzle over the chicken and vegetables.

Per serving: Calories: 400 kcal, Protein: 35 g, Carbohydrates: 35 g, Fats: 15 g, Fiber: 3 g, Sodium: Low

Chicken & Pea Linguine with Mascarpone Sauce

🕙 PREP: **10 mins** 🔍 COOK: **20 mins** 🍽 SERVES: **4**

Linguine: 12 ounces
Chicken Breast: 1 pound, thinly sliced
Sweet Peas: 1 cup (frozen or fresh)
Mascarpone Cheese: 1 cup
Garlic: 2 cloves, minced
Olive Oil: 2 tablespoons

1. Bring a large pot of salted water to a boil. Add the linguine and cook according to package instructions until al dente. Drain, reserving about 1 cup of the pasta water for later use.
2. While the pasta cooks, heat olive oil in a skillet over medium-high heat.
3. Add the minced garlic and sauté for about 1 minute until fragrant.
4. Add the thinly sliced chicken breast to the skillet. Season with salt and pepper. Cook, stirring occasionally, until the chicken is golden and cooked through about 6-8 minutes.
5. Add the sweet peas to the skillet with the chicken, and cook for 2-3 minutes until heated.
6. Reduce the heat to low and stir in the mascarpone cheese until it melts, creating a creamy sauce. If the sauce is too thick, add some reserved pasta water to reach your desired consistency.
7. Add the drained linguine to the skillet with the chicken and peas. Toss everything together until the pasta is evenly coated with the mascarpone sauce. Adjust seasoning with salt and pepper if needed.

Per serving: Calories: 750 kcal, Protein: 40 g, Carbohydrates: 70 g, Fats: 30 g, Fiber: 4 g, Sodium: Low

Deconstructed Lamb Gyros

⏰ PREP: **15 mins** 🍳 COOK: **10 mins** 🍽 SERVES: **4**

Ground Lamb: 1 pound
Pita Bread: 4 rounds
Tzatziki Sauce: 1 cup (store-bought or homemade from Greek yogurt, cucumber, garlic, and lemon juice)
Tomato: 1 large, diced
Red Onion: 1 small, thinly sliced
Olive Oil: For cooking

1. Heat a drizzle of olive oil in a skillet over medium-high heat.
Add the ground lamb, breaking it up with a spatula. Cook until browned and fully cooked through about 7-8 minutes. Season with salt and pepper to taste and any simple Greek seasonings you might have on hand (if within the ingredient limit).
2. While the lamb cooks, dice the tomato and thinly slice the red onion.
3. Warm the pita bread in the oven at 350°F for about 5 minutes, or lightly toast them in a dry skillet over medium heat for 30 seconds per side.
4. Lay out the warmed pita bread on plates.
5. Top each pita with a generous amount of cooked lamb, followed by the diced tomato and sliced red onion.

Per serving: Calories: 550 kcal, Protein: 28 g, Carbohydrates: 35 g, Fats: 32 g, Fiber: 2 g, Sodium: low

Grilled Chicken Chermoula Salad

⏰ PREP: **10 mins** 🍳 COOK: **10 mins** 🍽 SERVES: **4**

Chicken Breasts: 4 medium, boneless and skinless
Chermoula Paste: 1/4 cup (can be homemade or store-bought; parsley, garlic, cumin, coriander, lemon juice, and olive oil)
Mixed Salad Greens: 4 cups
Cherry Tomatoes: 1 cup, halved
Cucumber: 1 large, diced
Lemon: 1, for dressing and additional zest for garnish

1. Coat the chicken breasts generously with chermoula paste. Cover and refrigerate to marinate for at least 30 minutes or up to a few hours for more flavor.
2. Preheat the grill or grill pan to medium-high heat.
Grill the chicken breasts for 5 minutes on each side or until thoroughly cooked and the internal temperature reaches 165°F (75°C).
Once cooked, let the chicken rest for a few minutes before slicing it thinly.
3. Combine the mixed salad greens, halved cherry tomatoes, and diced cucumber in a large salad bowl.
4. Add the sliced grilled chicken on top of the green salad. Squeeze fresh lemon juice over the salad and toss gently to combine—season with salt and pepper to taste.

Per serving: Calories: 300 kcal, Protein: 35 g, Carbohydrates: 10 g, Fats: 15 g, Fiber: 3 g, Sodium: Low

Lamb & Apricot Skewers with Cucumber Mint Yogurt

⏰ PREP: **15 mins** 🔍 COOK: **15 mins** 🍽 SERVES: **4**

Lamb: 1 pound, cubed (shoulder or leg cut works well)
Dried Apricots: 1 cup, halved.
Greek Yogurt: 1 cup
Cucumber: 1 small, grated, and excess water squeezed out
Fresh Mint: A handful, chopped finely
Olive Oil: For brushing and marinating

1. Toss the lamb cubes with olive oil and salt in a bowl. To enhance flavor, let them marinate for at least 30 minutes in the refrigerator.
2. Combine the Greek yogurt, grated cucumber, and chopped mint in a small bowl. Mix thoroughly to blend the flavors. Refrigerate until ready to serve.
3. Thread the marinated lamb cubes and halved dried apricots onto the skewers, alternating between lamb and apricots.
4. Preheat the grill or grill pan over medium-high heat.
Brush the grill with a bit of olive oil to prevent sticking.
Grill the skewers, turning occasionally, until the lamb is cooked to the desired doneness, about 8-10 minutes for medium-rare.

Per serving: Calories: 350 kcal, Protein: 25 g, Carbohydrates: 20 g, Fats: 20 g, Fiber: 2 g, Sodium: Low

Shish Tawook with Garlic Sauce

⏰ PREP: **10 mins** 🔍 COOK: **10 mins** 🍽 SERVES: **4**

Chicken Breast: 1.5 pounds, cut into cubes
Plain Yogurt: 1/2 cup
Garlic: 4 cloves, minced
Lemon Juice: 2 tablespoons
Paprika: 1 teaspoon
Salt and Pepper: To taste

1. Combine the plain yogurt, minced garlic, lemon juice, paprika, salt, and pepper in a mixing bowl.
2. Add the chicken cubes to the marinade, ensuring each piece is well coated. Cover and refrigerate for at least 1 hour or overnight for best results.
3. Combine the garlic cloves and salt in a food processor or blender. Blend until the garlic is finely minced.
4. Slowly add the lemon juice and olive oil while blending until the mixture becomes creamy and emulsified.
5. Preheat the grill or grill pan over medium-high heat.
6. Thread the marinated chicken cubes onto skewers.
7. Grill the skewers, turning occasionally, until the chicken is fully cooked and has excellent grill marks, about 10-15 minutes.

Per serving: Calories: 400 kcal, Protein: 38 g, Carbohydrates: 5 g, Fats: 24 g, Fiber: 1 g, Sodium: Low

Smoky Braised Chicken & Artichokes

⏰ PREP: **10 mins** ◷ COOK: **45 mins** 🍽 SERVES: **4**

Chicken Thighs: 8 pieces (bone-in, skin-on for more flavor)
Artichoke Hearts: 1 can (14 ounces), drained
Smoked Paprika: 2 teaspoons
Chicken Broth: 2 cups
Garlic: 4 cloves, minced
Olive Oil: 2 tablespoons

1. Heat the olive oil in a large skillet or Dutch oven over medium-high heat.
2. Season the chicken thighs with salt and smoked paprika.
3. Place the chicken, skin-side down, in the skillet and cook until the skin is golden and crispy about 5-7 minutes. Flip and cook for another 5 minutes.
4. Remove chicken from the skillet and set aside.
5. Reduce the heat to medium. Add the minced garlic to the remaining oil in the skillet and sauté for about 1 minute until fragrant.
6. Add the artichoke hearts to the skillet and stir to mix with the garlic. Pour in the chicken broth and bring to a simmer.
7. Return the chicken thighs to the skillet, skin-side up. Cover and let the chicken simmer gently for about 30 minutes or until it is thoroughly cooked and tender.
Per serving: Calories: 450 kcal, Protein: 35 g, Carbohydrates: 8 g, Fats: 32 g, Fiber: 3 g, Sodium: Moderate

Dukkah Chicken Breasts

⏰ PREP: **10 mins** ◷ COOK: **10 mins** 🍽 SERVES: **4**

Chicken Breasts: 4, boneless and skinless
Dukkah: 1/4 cup (store-bought or homemade with nuts like hazelnuts or almonds, sesame seeds, coriander, and cumin)
Olive Oil: 2 tablespoons, plus extra for cooking
Lemon Juice: 2 tablespoons (to help the dukkah adhere and add flavor)
Salt and Pepper: To taste

1. If the chicken breasts are very thick, gently pound them to an even thickness using a meat mallet or rolling pin. This helps ensure even cooking and tenderizes the meat.
2. Season the chicken breasts with salt and pepper.
3. Brush the chicken breasts with olive oil and lemon juice. This adds flavor and helps the dukkah stick to the chicken.
4. Coat the chicken breasts generously with dukkah, pressing it into the meat to adhere well.
5. To Bake: Preheat the oven to 375°F (190°C). Place the dukkah-coated chicken breasts on a greased baking sheet and bake for 20-25 minutes until the chicken is thoroughly cooked and the juices run clear.
6. To Pan-Fry: Heat a tablespoon of olive oil in a large skillet over medium heat. Add the chicken and cook for about 5-7 minutes on each side until golden brown is cooked through.
Per serving: Calories: 280 kcal, Protein: 26 g, Carbohydrates: 3 g, Fats: 18 g, Fiber: 1 g, Sodium: Low

Moroccan-spiced skillet Chicken and Couscous

🕐 PREP: **15 mins** 🔍 COOK: **20 mins** 🍽 SERVES: **4**

Chicken Breasts: 4, boneless and skinless
Moroccan Spice Mix: 2 tablespoons (a blend of cumin, corian-
der, cinnamon, paprika, and turmeric)
Couscous: 1 cup
Chicken Broth: 2 cups (to cook the couscous and add extra fla-
vor)
Raisins or Dried Apricots: 1/2 cup (for sweetness and texture)

1. Pat the chicken breasts dry with paper towels. Rub each breast with the Moroccan spice mix, ensuring they are well-coated. Let sit for a few minutes.
2. Heat a tablespoon of oil in a large skillet over medium-high heat. Once hot, add the chicken breasts. Cook for 5-7 minutes on each side until golden brown and cooked through. Remove from the skillet and set aside.
3. In the same skillet, add the chicken broth and bring it to a boil. Stir in the couscous and dried fruit (raisins or chopped dried apricots). Cover and remove from heat. Let it sit for about 5 minutes until the couscous has absorbed all the liquid and is tender.
4. Fluff the couscous with a fork and mix in half of the chopped cilantro or parsley. Slice the chicken breasts and lay them over the couscous.
Per serving: Calories: 450 kcal, Protein: 35 g, Carbohydrates: 40 g, Fats: 15 g, Fiber: 3 g, Sodium: Low

Paprika Chicken with Crispy Chickpeas & Tomatoes

🕐 PREP: **10 mins** 🔍 COOK: **25 mins** 🍽 SERVES: **4**

Chicken Thighs: 4, bone-in and skin-on
Smoked Paprika: 2 tablespoons
Chickpeas: 1 can (15 ounces), drained, rinsed, and dried
Cherry Tomatoes: 1 cup
Olive Oil: 3 tablespoons
Salt and Pepper: To taste

1. Preheat your oven to 425°F (220°C).
2. Toss the chicken thighs with half the olive oil, smoked paprika, salt, and pepper until well-coated in a large bowl.
Toss the chickpeas with the remaining olive oil and a pinch of salt in the same or a separate bowl.
3. Place the chicken thighs skin-side up on a large baking sheet.
Spread the chickpeas around the chicken on the baking sheet.
4. Place the baking sheet in the oven and roast for about 20 minutes.
After 20 minutes, add the cherry tomatoes to the baking sheet, tossing them lightly with the chickpeas. Continue to roast for another 5-10 minutes until the chicken is thoroughly cooked (internal temperature reaches 165°F or 74°C) and the skin is crispy.
5. Remove from the oven. Let the chicken rest for a few minutes before serving.
6. Serve the chicken thighs with a hearty scoop of crispy chickpeas and roasted tomatoes.
Per serving: Calories: 550 kcal, Protein: 35 g, Carbohydrates: 20 g, Fats: 35 g, Fiber: 5 g, Sodium: Low

Sticky Grilled Chicken with Corn & Potatoes

⏰ PREP: **10 mins** ⏱ COOK: **30 mins** 🍽 SERVES: **4**

Chicken Thighs: 8 pieces, bone-in, and skin-on for more flavor
BBQ Sauce: 1 cup (choose a sticky variety like a honey BBQ for best results)
Corn on the Cob: 4 ears, husked
Baby Potatoes: 1 pound, halved or quartered depending on size
Olive Oil: 2 tablespoons
Salt and Pepper: To taste

1. Toss the halved baby potatoes with one tablespoon of olive oil, salt, and pepper.
2. Wrap the potatoes in aluminum foil, creating a foil packet.
Place the foil packet on the grill over indirect heat and cook for about 25-30 minutes, turning occasionally, until the potatoes are tender.
3. Preheat the grill to medium-high heat. Place the chicken thighs on the grill, skin-side down first, grilling for 6-7 minutes per side. During the last few minutes of cooking, baste the chicken with the remaining BBQ sauce, turning frequently to prevent burning.
4. Cook until the internal temperature reaches 165°F (75°C).
5. Brush the corn with olive oil and season with salt and pepper.
6. Place the corn directly on the grill, turning occasionally, about 10-12 minutes.

Per serving: Calories: 650 kcal, Protein: 35 g, Carbohydrates: 55 g, Fats: 35 g, Fiber: 5 g, Sodium: Moderate

Chicken à l'Orange

⏰ PREP: **10 mins** ⏱ COOK: **30 mins** 🍽 SERVES: **4**

Chicken Breasts: 4, boneless and skinless
Orange Juice: 1 cup (preferably freshly squeezed for better flavor)
Chicken Broth: 1/2 cup
Orange Zest: From 1 orange
Sugar: 2 tablespoons

1. Preheat your oven to 375°F (190°C).
2. Heat the butter over medium-high heat in an oven-proof skillet until melted and foamy.
3. Season the chicken breasts with salt and pepper, then place them in the skillet. Cook until golden brown on each side, about 3-4 minutes per side. Remove the chicken from the skillet and set aside.
4. In the same skillet, reduce the heat to medium. Add the orange juice, chicken broth, and sugar. Bring to a simmer, whisking frequently, until the sugar is dissolved. Add the orange zest, and let the sauce simmer for about 5 minutes or until it thickens slightly.
5. Return the chicken breasts to the skillet with the orange sauce. Transfer the skillet to the preheated oven and bake for 15-20 minutes.
6. Plate the chicken breasts and spoon the thickened orange sauce over them. If desired, garnish with additional orange zest or a slice of orange. Serve hot, ideally with a side of rice or steamed vegetables to soak up the extra sauce.

Per serving: Calories: 290 kcal, Protein: 26 g, Carbohydrates: 15 g, Fats: 12 g, Fiber: 0 g, Sodium: Low

Fried Chicken with Lemony Roasted Broccoli

⏰ PREP: **15 mins** 🔍 COOK: **25 mins** 🍽 SERVES: **4**

Chicken Breasts: 4 boneless and skinless
Broccoli Florets: 4 cups
Lemon: 1, zest and juice
Olive Oil: 3 tablespoons (divided for chicken and broccoli)
Salt and Pepper: To taste
Garlic Powder: 1 teaspoon (for added flavor to both chicken and broccoli)

1. Preheat the oven to 425°F (220°C).
2. In a mixing bowl, toss the broccoli florets with two tablespoons of olive oil, half lemon zest, half lemon juice, garlic powder, salt, and pepper.
3. Spread the broccoli on a baking sheet in a single layer.
4. Roast in the oven for about 20-25 minutes until the edges are crispy.
5. While the broccoli is roasting, season the chicken breasts with salt, pepper, and garlic powder.
6. Heat the remaining tablespoon of olive oil in a large skillet over medium-high heat.
7. Add the chicken breasts to the skillet and cook for 5-7 minutes on each side or until golden brown and cooked through.
8. Once the broccoli is roasted, sprinkle it with the remaining lemon zest and lemon juice.

Per serving: Calories: 300 kcal, Protein: 26 g, Carbohydrates: 8 g, Fats: 18 g, Fiber: 3 g, Sodium: Low

Chicken Shawarma

⏰ PREP: **15 mins** 🔍 COOK: **20 mins** 🍽 SERVES: **4**

Chicken Thighs: 1.5 pounds, boneless and skinless
Yogurt: 1/2 cup (helps tenderize the meat)
Lemon Juice: 2 tablespoons
Garlic: 4 cloves, minced
Shawarma Spice Blend: 2 tablespoons (typically includes cumin, coriander, paprika, turmeric, and cinnamon)
Olive Oil: 2 tablespoons

1. Combine the yogurt, lemon juice, minced garlic, shawarma spice blend, and olive oil in a large mixing bowl. Mix well to create the marinade.
2. Add the chicken thighs to the marinade, ensuring each piece is thoroughly coated. Cover and refrigerate for at least 1 hour or overnight for best results.
3. For Grilling, Preheat your grill to medium-high heat. Remove the chicken from the marinade, letting excess drip off. Grill the chicken on each side for 5-7 minutes or until fully cooked and slightly charred.
4. Preheat your oven to 425°F (220°C). Line a baking sheet with aluminum foil and place the chicken on it. Bake for about 20 minutes until the chicken is cooked through and the edges begin to crisp.
5. Let the chicken rest for a few minutes after cooking, then slice it thinly to mimic the texture of traditional shawarma.

Per serving: Calories: 400 kcal, Protein: 35 g, Carbohydrates: 5 g, Fats: 25 g, Fiber: 1 g, Sodium: Low

Seared Chicken with Cheesy Spinach & Artichokes

⏰ PREP: **10 mins** ⏱ COOK: **20 mins** 🍽 SERVES: **4**

Chicken Breasts: 4, boneless and skinless
Spinach: 2 cups, fresh (or you can substitute with frozen, thawed and drained)
Artichoke Hearts: 1 can (14 ounces), drained and chopped
Cream Cheese: 1/2 cup
Parmesan Cheese: 1/2 cup, grated
Olive Oil: 2 tablespoons

1. Season the chicken breasts with salt and pepper.
2. Heat olive oil in a large skillet over medium-high heat. Once hot, add the chicken breasts. Cook for about 5-7 minutes on each side or until golden brown and cooked through (internal temperature should reach 165°F).
3. In the same skillet, reduce heat to medium.
4. Add the cream cheese and stir until melted and smooth.
5. Stir in the chopped artichoke hearts and spinach. Continue cooking and stirring until the spinach is wilted and everything is well combined.
6. Sprinkle with grated Parmesan cheese and stir until the cheese is melted and the mixture is creamy.
7. Return the seared chicken to the skillet, spooning the cheesy spinach and artichoke mixture over the chicken. Cook for 2-3 minutes on low heat to reheat the chicken and meld the flavors together.
Per serving: Calories: 300 kcal, Protein: 5 g, Carbohydrates: 5 g, Fats: 30 g, Fiber: 0 g, Sodium: Low

Chicken & Eggplant Cutlets

⏰ PREP: **10 mins** ⏱ COOK: **15 mins** 🍽 SERVES: **4**

Chicken Breasts: 2 large, thinly sliced or pounded thin
Eggplant: 1 large, sliced into 1/4 inch thick rounds
Breadcrumbs: 1 cup (for coating)
Eggs: 2, beaten (for dredging)
Parmesan Cheese: 1/2 cup, grated (mixed into breadcrumbs for flavor)
Olive Oil: for frying

1. Set up two shallow dishes. Beat the eggs in the first, and mix the breadcrumbs with grated Parmesan cheese in the second.
2. Season the chicken breasts and eggplant slices with salt and pepper. Dip each piece of chicken and eggplant first into the beaten eggs, then coat them thoroughly in the breadcrumb-Parmesan mixture.
3. Heat olive oil in a large skillet over medium-high heat.
Once the oil is hot, add the breaded chicken and eggplant cutlets, cooking in batches to avoid overcrowding the pan.
4. Cook each cutlet for about 3-4 minutes per side or until golden brown and the chicken is cooked.
5. Transfer the cooked cutlets to a plate lined with paper towels to drain excess oil.
6. Serve the chicken and eggplant cutlets hot. They pair well with a side salad, a squeeze of lemon for added zest, or a light tomato sauce if desired.
Per serving: Calories: 400 kcal, Protein: 30 g, Carbohydrates: 20 g, Fats: 20 g, Fiber: 3 g, Sodium:

Pork Chops & Fried Peppers

⏰ PREP: **15 mins** 🍳 COOK: **20 mins** 🍽️ SERVES: **4**

Pork Chops: 4 bone-in or boneless
Bell Peppers: 2 large, sliced (use a mix of colors for visual appeal, like red and yellow)
Onion: 1 large, sliced
Garlic: 2 cloves, minced
Olive Oil: 3 tablespoons
Salt and Pepper: To taste

1. Season the pork chops with salt and pepper on both sides. Slice the bell peppers and onion. Mince the garlic.
2. Heat 2 tablespoons of olive oil in a large skillet over medium-high heat.
3. Add the pork chops to the skillet. Cook for about 4-5 minutes per side or until they reach an internal temperature of 145°F (63°C) and are nicely browned. Remove the pork chops from the skillet and set aside to rest.
4. In the same skillet, add the remaining tablespoon of olive oil. Add the sliced onions and peppers, sautéing until they soften, about 5 mis.
5. Add the minced garlic and cook for 1-2 minutes, until fragrant.
6. Return the pork chops to the skillet with the peppers and onions. Cook together for a couple of minutes to reheat the pork chops and mingle the flavors.
7. Adjust seasoning with additional salt and pepper if needed.
Per serving: Calories: 350 kcal, Protein: 25 g, Carbohydrates: 8 g, Fats: 25 g, Fiber: 2 g, Sodium: Low

Ham & Fontina Lasagna

⏰ PREP: **15 mins** 🍳 COOK: **40 mins** 🍽️ SERVES: **4**

Lasagna Noodles: 9-12 sheets, depending on your pan size (pre-cooked or no-boil for convenience)
Fontina Cheese: 2 cups, grated
Cooked Ham: 1.5 cups, diced
Ricotta Cheese: 1 cup
Milk: 1 cup (to help form a light sauce with the ricotta)
Salt and Pepper: To taste

1. Preheat your oven to 375°F (190°C).
2. Mix the ricotta cheese with milk, salt, and pepper until smooth in a mixing bowl. This mixture will help create a creamy layer between the noodles.
3. Spread a thin layer of the ricotta mixture at the bottom of the baking dish. Place a layer of lasagna noodles over the ricotta.
4. Spread a layer of the ricotta mixture over the noodles, then sprinkle with a third of the diced ham and a third of the grated Fontina cheese.
5. Repeat the layering process (noodles, ricotta mixture, ham, Fontina) twice, ending with a generous layer of Fontina cheese.
6. Cover the baking dish with aluminum foil and bake in the oven for 30 minutes. Remove the foil and continue baking for another 10 minutes until the top is bubbly and golden.
7. After removing the lasagna from the oven, let it sit for 10 minutes to set up, making it easier to slice. Cut into squares and serve warm.
Per serving: Calories: 450 kcal, Protein: 28 g, Carbohydrates: 35 g, Fats: 22 g, Fiber: 2 g, Sodium: Moderate

Rabbit in a Red Sauce

⏰ PREP: **10 mins** ◎ COOK: **1 hour** 🍽 SERVES: **4**

Rabbit: 1 whole rabbit (about 2 to 3 pounds), cut into pieces.
Tomato Sauce: 2 cups, either homemade
Onion: 1 large, finely chopped
Garlic: 3 cloves, minced
Olive Oil: 2 tablespoons

1.Pat the rabbit pieces dry and season generously with salt and pepper.
2. Heat the olive oil in a large pot or Dutch oven over medium-high heat. Add the rabbit pieces and sear them until golden brown on all sides, about 5-7 minutes per side. Remove the rabbit and set it aside on a plate.
3. Reduce the heat to medium in the same pot and add the chopped onion. Sauté until the onion is soft and translucent, about 5 minutes.
4. Add the minced garlic and cook for another 1-2 minutes until fragrant.
5. Return the rabbit to the pot and pour in the tomato sauce. Stir well to combine and ensure the rabbit is well coated with the sauce.
6. Bring the mixture to a simmer, then cover and reduce the heat to low. Let the rabbit cook slowly for about 1 hour or until the meat is tender and quickly pulls away from the bone.
7. Check the seasoning and adjust with more salt and pepper if needed. Serve the rabbit in its sauce, ideally with simple steamed vegetables, mashed potatoes, or rustic bread to soak up the delicious sauce.
Per serving: Calories: 400 kcal, Protein: 35 g, Carbohydrates: 10 g, Fats: 20 g, Fiber: 2 g, Sodium: Moderate

Rabbit with Yogurt

⏰ PREP: **15 mins** ◎ COOK: **1 hour** 🍽 SERVES: **4**

Rabbit: 1 whole rabbit (about 2 to 3 pounds), cut into serving pieces.
Plain Yogurt: 1 cup (use full-fat yogurt for best results)
Garlic: 4 cloves, minced
Olive Oil: 2 tablespoons
Lemon Juice: 2 tablespoons (to brighten the sauce)
Salt and Pepper: To taste

1. Preheat your oven to 350°F (175°C).
2. Combine the yogurt, minced garlic, lemon juice, salt, and pepper in a bowl.
3. Place the rabbit pieces in a large bowl or plastic bag. Pour the yogurt marinade over the rabbit, ensuring all pieces are well-coated. Let the rabbit marinate for at least 30 minutes, or for better flavor absorption, marinate in the refrigerator for a few hours or overnight.
4. Heat olive oil over medium-high heat in a large oven-proof skillet. Remove the rabbit from the marinade, shaking off excess. Brown the rabbit pieces on all sides in the skillet, about 2-3 minutes per side. Once browned, pour the remaining yogurt marinade over the rabbit.
5. Cover the skillet with aluminum foil or a lid and place it in the oven. Bake for about 45 minutes to 1 hour until the rabbit is tender, and the sauce has thickened slightly.
6. Check the seasoning and adjust with additional salt and pepper if needed.
7. Serve hot, garnished with a sprinkle of fresh herbs like parsley or thyme if desired.
Per serving: Calories: 400 kcal, Protein: 35 g, Carbohydrates: 5 g, Fats: 25 g, Fiber: 0 g, Sodium: Low

Lamb with Okra

⏰ PREP: **15 mins** 🔍 COOK: **1 hour** 🍽 SERVES: **4**

Lamb Shoulder: 1.5 pounds, cut into 1-inch cubes
Okra: 1 pound, tops trimmed
Tomatoes: 2 large, diced (or one can of diced tomatoes)
Onion: 1 large, finely chopped
Garlic: 3 cloves, minced
Olive Oil: 2 tablespoons

1. Heat the olive oil in a large pot or Dutch oven over medium-high heat. Add the lamb cubes and season with salt and pepper. Brown the lamb on all sides, about 5-7 minutes. Remove the lamb from the pot and set aside.
2. In the same pot, add the chopped onion and minced garlic. Sauté until the onion is translucent and soft, about 5 minutes.
3. Add the diced tomatoes, stirring to combine and scraping any browned bits from the bottom of the pot.
4. Return the lamb to the pot. Add the okra around the lamb.
5. Cover and simmer over low heat for about 45-50 minutes, or until the lamb is tender and the okra is cooked but still holds its shape.

Per serving: Calories: 400 kcal, Protein: 35 g, Carbohydrates: 15 g, Fats: 25 g, Fiber: 5 g, Sodium: Low

Browned Lamb

⏰ PREP: **15 mins** 🔍 COOK: **20 mins** 🍽 SERVES: **4**

Lamb: 1 pound of lamb cut of choice (e.g., chops, cubes for stew)
Olive Oil: 1 tablespoon
Salt: 1 teaspoon
Pepper: ½ teaspoon

1. Combine the yogurt, lemon juice, minced garlic, shawarma spice blend, anPat the lamb dry with paper towels. This helps achieve a better search. Season all sides of the lamb generously with salt and pepper.
2. Place your skillet over medium-high heat and let it get hot.
Add the olive oil to the skillet. It should shimmer, indicating it is ready for searing.
3. Place the lamb in the hot skillet. Let it cook undisturbed for about 3-4 minutes on each side for chops or 1-2 minutes per side for smaller pieces like cubes.
4. The lamb should develop a rich, golden-brown crust. Flip only once to ensure even browning.
5. For chops, ensure the medium-rare internal temperature reaches 145°F. For cubes, ensure they are browned all around and slightly firm to the touch.
6. Remove the lamb from the skillet and rest for about 5 minutes. This helps redistribute the juices inside the meat, making it more tender.

Per serving: Calories: 250 kcal, Protein: 22 g, Total Fat: 18 g, Saturated Fat: 7 g, Carbohydrates: 0 g

Lamb Fricassee

⏰ PREP: **10 mins** 🍳 COOK: **1 hours** 🍽 SERVES: **4**

Lamb Shoulder: 1.5 pounds, cut into chunks
Onions: 1 large, finely chopped
Chicken Broth: 2 cups
Flour: 2 tablespoons (to thicken the sauce)
Lemon Juice: 2 tablespoons (for a touch of acidity)
Olive Oil: 2 tablespoons

1. Heat olive oil in a large pot or Dutch oven over medium-high heat. Pat the lamb dry and season it with salt and pepper. Add the lamb to the pot and sear until it's browned on all sides, about 5-7 minutes. Remove the lamb and set it aside.
2. Reduce the heat to medium in the same pot and add the chopped onions. Cook until they are soft and translucent, about 5 minutes.
3. Sprinkle the flour over the onions, stir well, and cook for another minute to remove the raw flour taste. Gradually stir in the chicken broth, ensuring there are no lumps. Bring to a simmer.
4. Return the lamb to the pot. Cover and simmer on low heat for about 45 minutes or until tender.
5. Stir in the lemon juice once the lamb is tender, and adjust the seasoning with additional salt and pepper.
Per serving: Calories: 400 kcal, Protein: 30 g, Carbohydrates: 10 g, Fats: 25 g, Fiber: 1 g, Sodium: Low

Lamb Ofto (Antikristo)

⏰ PREP: **15 mins** 🍳 COOK: **2 hours** 🍽 SERVES: **4**

Lamb Shoulder: 2 pounds, cut into large chunks
Olive Oil: 2 tablespoons for coating the lamb
Salt: 2 teaspoons, or to taste
Fresh Rosemary: 2 sprigs or one teaspoon of dried rosemary
Garlic: 4 cloves, minced
Lemon: 1, juiced (to finish the dish before serving)

1. Preheat your oven to 325°F (165°C). This low and slow method will help tenderize the lamb.
2. Pat the lamb dry with paper towels. This helps to achieve a crispier surface.
3. Rub the lamb pieces with olive oil, then season generously with salt, minced garlic, and rosemary. Ensure the lamb is evenly coated with the seasoning.
4. Place the seasoned lamb in a roasting pan. Arrange it so that each piece has some space around it; this helps the heat circulate and brown the meat evenly.
5. Roast in the preheated oven for about 1.5 to 2 hours. During the last 30 minutes of cooking, you can increase the oven temperature to 375°F if you prefer a more charred exterior.
6. Please remove it from the oven once the lamb is cooked and the outside is nicely browned and crisp.
7. Squeeze fresh lemon juice over the hot lamb to add freshness and cut through the meat's richness.
Per serving: Calories: 450 kcal, Protein: 38 g, Carbohydrates: 1 g, Fats: 32 g, Fiber: 0 g, Sodium: Low

Lamb with Cream Wrapped in Phyllo

🕐 PREP: **20 mins** 🎯 COOK: **25 mins** 🍽 SERVES: **4**

Lamb: 1 pound, ground
Heavy Cream: 1/2 cup
Phyllo Dough Sheets: 8 sheets
Butter: 4 tablespoons, melted (for brushing phyllo)
Onion: 1 small, finely chopped
Salt and Pepper: To taste

1. Heat a skillet over medium heat. Add the finely chopped onion and sauté until translucent.
2. Add the ground lamb to the skillet. Cook until browned and no longer pink, breaking it up with a spatula as it cooks—season with salt and pepper. Stir in the heavy cream and cook for 2-3 minutes until the mixture thickens.
3. Preheat your oven to 375°F (190°C). Lay out a sheet of phyllo dough on a clean work surface. Brush lightly with melted butter. Place another sheet on top and brush again with butter. Repeat until you have four layers.
4. Divide the lamb and cream mixture evenly between the two sets of phyllo layers. Fold the phyllo over the lamb mixture to create a parcel. Tuck in the edges to seal the filling inside. Place the phyllo parcels on a baking sheet lined with parchment paper. Brush the tops with the remaining melted butter.Bake in the oven for 20-25 minutes.

Per serving: Calories: 550 kcal, Protein: 22 g, Carbohydrates: 20 g, Fats: 40 g, Fiber: 1 g, Sodium: Low

Lamb with Vegetables and Yogurt

🕐 PREP: **15 mins** 🎯 COOK: **30 mins** 🍽 SERVES: **4**

Lamb: 1.5 pounds, cut into cubes (leg or shoulder works well)
Mixed Vegetables: 3 cups (such as bell peppers, zucchini, and cherry tomatoes)
Plain Yogurt: 1 cup (use Greek yogurt for a thicker consistency)
Garlic: 2 cloves, minced (for the yogurt sauce)
Olive Oil: 2 tablespoons (for cooking)
Salt and Pepper: To taste

1. Mix the plain yogurt with minced garlic and a pinch of salt in a small bowl. Set aside to let the flavors meld.
2. Heat the olive oil in a large skillet over medium-high heat. Season the lamb cubes with salt and pepper. Add them to the skillet and cook until browned on all sides and nearly cooked through, about 8-10 minutes. Remove the lamb from the skillet and set aside.
3. In the same skillet, add the mixed vegetables. Season with a bit of salt and pepper. Sauté until they are tender but still crisp, about 5-7 minutes. You can adjust the cooking time based on how tender you like your vegetables.
4. Return the lamb to the skillet with the vegetables, stirring to combine. Cook for another 2-3 minutes to ensure the lamb is cooked through and the flavors are combined.

Per serving: Calories: 450 kcal, Protein: 35 g, Carbohydrates: 12 g, Fats: 30 g, Fiber: 3 g, Sodium: Low

Lamb with Artichokes, Egg, and Lemon

⏰ PREP: **15 mins** ◎ COOK: **45 mins** 🍽 SERVES: **4**

Lamb Shoulder: 1.5 pounds, cut into cubes
Artichoke Hearts: 1 can (14 ounces), drained and quartered
Eggs: 2 large
Lemon Juice: From 1 lemon
Olive Oil: 2 tablespoons
Salt and Pepper: To taste

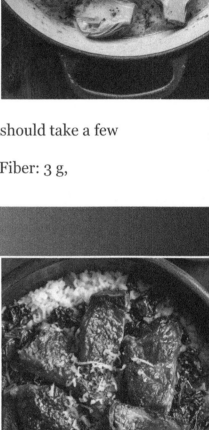

1. Heat the olive oil in a large skillet or Dutch oven over medium-high heat.
2. Season the lamb cubes with salt and pepper, then add them to the skillet.
3. Brown the lamb on all sides, about 5-7 minutes. Remove the lamb from the skillet and set aside.
4. Add the artichoke hearts and sauté in the same skillet for a few minutes until they get some color.
5. Return the lamb to the skillet with the artichokes. Add enough water to cover the ingredients halfway, simmer, and cook for about 30-35 minutes.
6. Whisk the eggs with the lemon juice in a mixing bowl until well combined.
7. Once the lamb is tender, reduce the heat to low. Slowly drizzle the egg and lemon mixture into the skillet, stirring constantly, until the sauce thickens. This should take a few minutes. Be careful not to boil the sauce to prevent the eggs from scrambling.

Per serving: Calories: 450 kcal, Protein: 35 g, Carbohydrates: 10 g, Fats: 30 g, Fiber: 3 g, Sodium: Moderate

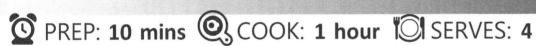

Sinklina

⏰ PREP: **10 mins** ◎ COOK: **1 hour** 🍽 SERVES: **4**

Cured Lamb: 1.5 pounds (traditionally, the lamb should be salted and cured for several days)
Swiss Chard: 1 bunch, chopped (or other greens like spinach or collard greens)
Onion: 1 large, chopped
Rice: 1/2 cup, uncooked
Lemon Juice: From 1 lemon
Olive Oil: 2 tablespoons

1. If you have access to pre-cured lamb, that's perfect; otherwise, you may need to prepare this for several days by rubbing lamb with salt and letting it cure in the refrigerator.
2. Heat the olive oil in a large pot over medium heat. Add the chopped onion and sauté until it becomes translucent. Add the cured lamb to the pot and cover with water. Bring to a boil, then reduce heat and simmer for about 45 minutes or until the lamb is tender.
3. Add the chopped Swiss chard and rice to the pot. Continue to cook for another 15 minutes or until the rice and greens are tender.
4. Stir in the lemon juice once the dish is cooked for a fresh, zesty finish.

Per serving: Calories: 350 kcal, Protein: 25 g, Carbohydrates: 15 g, Fats: 20 g, Fiber: 2 g, Sodium: Low

Grilled Pork and Smoky Corn Salad

🕐 PREP: **15 mins** 🔍 COOK: **25 mins** 🍽 SERVES: **4**

Pork Chops: 4 medium (about 1 pound)
Corn on the Cob: 4 ears, husked
Olive Oil: 2 tablespoons (for brushing)
Salt and Pepper: To taste
Lime: 1, juiced
Fresh Cilantro: 1/4 cup, chopped (for garnish and added flavor)

1. Preheat your grill to medium-high heat.
2. Brush the pork chops and corn with olive oil—season generously with salt and pepper.
3. Place the pork chops and corn on the grill. Grill the pork chops for about 4-5 minutes per side or until they reach an internal temperature of 145°F (63°C) and are nicely charred.
4. Turn the corn occasionally, grilling it until charred on all sides, about 10-12 minutes.
5. Once the corn is cool enough to handle, cut the kernels off the cobs into a bowl.
6. Add the lime juice and half of the chopped cilantro to the corn and mix well.

Per serving: Calories: 350 kcal, Protein: 30 g, Carbohydrates: 25 g, Fats: 15 g, Fiber: 3 g, Sodium: Low

Roasted Butternut Squash and Pork Chops

🕐 PREP: **15 mins** 🔍 COOK: **30 mins** 🍽 SERVES: **4**

Pork Chops: 4 bone-in or boneless (about 1 pound total)
Butternut Squash: 1 medium, peeled, seeded, and cubed
Olive Oil: 2 tablespoons
Salt and Pepper: To taste
Garlic Powder: 1 teaspoon
Fresh Thyme: 1 tablespoon, chopped (or one teaspoon dried thyme)

1. Preheat your oven to 425°F.
2. In a large bowl, toss the cubed butternut squash with half of the olive oil, salt, pepper, garlic powder, and half of the thyme. Rub the pork chops in another bowl with the remaining olive oil, salt, pepper, and the rest of the thyme.
3. Spread the seasoned butternut squash on a baking sheet lined with aluminum foil or parchment paper. Roast in the preheated oven for about 15 minutes.
4. After the squash has roasted for 15 minutes, stir it around and make space on the baking sheet to add the pork chops.
5. Place the pork chops on the baking sheet with the squash and return to the oven. Roast for 10-15 minutes, or until the pork chops are cooked through and the squash is tender and caramelized.
6. Serve the pork chops alongside the roasted butternut squash. Garnish with additional thyme if desired.

Per serving: Calories: 350 kcal, Protein: 28 g, Carbohydrates: 25 g, Fats: 15 g, Fiber: 5 g, Sodium: Moderate

Steak with Harissa Butter Carrots

⏰ PREP: **10 mins** ⌚ COOK: **20 mins** 🍽 SERVES: **4**

Steaks: 4 (ribeye, sirloin, or your choice, about 6-8 ounces each)
Carrots: 1 pound, peeled and sliced diagonally
Harissa Paste: 2 tablespoons
Butter: 2 tablespoons
Salt and Pepper: To taste
Olive Oil: 1 tablespoon (for grilling or pan-searing the steaks)

1. Preheat your oven to 400°F (200°C) to roast the carrots.
2. Mix the harissa paste with the butter in a small bowl until well combined. Toss the sliced carrots in the harissa butter mixture until evenly coated— season with salt.
3. Spread the carrots on a baking sheet or in a roasting pan. Roast in the oven for about 20 minutes or until tender and slightly caramelized, stirring halfway through for even cooking.
4. While the carrots are roasting, season the steaks generously with salt and pepper. Heat the olive oil in a skillet.
5. Cook the steaks to your desired level of doneness, approximately 3-4 minutes per side for medium-rare, depending on the thickness. Remove the steaks from the heat and let them rest for a few minutes before serving. This helps retain the juices and flavors.

Per serving: Calories: 450 kcal, Protein: 35 g, Carbohydrates: 15 g, Fats: 30 g, Fiber: 4 g, Sodium: Low

Steak with Farro Salad and Grilled Green Beans

⏰ PREP: **10 mins** ⌚ COOK: **15 mins** 🍽 SERVES: **4**

Steaks: 4 (such as sirloin or ribeye, about 6-8 ounces each)
Farro: 1 cup, uncooked
Green Beans: 1 pound, ends trimmed
Olive Oil: For drizzling
Salt and Pepper: To taste
Lemon Juice: From 1 lemon (to dress the salad)

1. Rinse the farro under cold water.
2. Bring a saucepan of salted water to a boil and add the farro. Reduce heat to a simmer and cook until the farro is tender but still chewy about 15-20 minutes.
3. Drain any excess water and let cool slightly.
4. While the farro is cooking, preheat your grill or grill pan to medium-high heat. Toss the green beans with olive oil, salt, and pepper.
5. Grill the green beans for about 5-7 minutes, turning occasionally, until they are tender and have grill marks.
6. Season the steaks with salt and pepper. Grill the steaks to your desired doneness, about 3-4 minutes per side for medium-rare, depending on thickness. Remove from the grill and let rest for a few minutes.
7. Combine the cooked farro with lemon juice and a drizzle of olive oil, salt, and pepper in a mixing bowl. Adjust seasoning to taste.

Per serving: Calories: 550 kcal, Protein: 40 g, Carbohydrates: 45 g, Fats: 22 g, Fiber: 8 g, Sodium: Moderate

Pierogi with Sautéed Cabbage

🕐 PREP: **15 mins** 🍳 COOK: **20 mins** 🍽 SERVES: **4**

Pierogi: 24 store-bought or homemade, filled with your choice of cheese, potato, or meat
Cabbage: 1 medium head, thinly sliced
Butter: 4 tablespoons
Onion: 1 large, thinly sliced
Salt and Pepper: To taste
Vinegar (optional): 1 tablespoon apple cider or white (to enhance the flavor of the cabbage)

1. Bring a large pot of salted water to a boil. Add the pierogi to the boiling water and cook according to package instructions or until they float to the top and are cooked through, typically about 5 minutes for fresh or frozen.
2. Melt two tablespoons of butter in a large skillet over medium heat.
3. Add the sliced onion to the skillet and sauté until the onion becomes translucent, about 3-4 minutes. Add the sliced cabbage to the skillet, stirring to mix with the onions—season with salt and pepper.
4. Cook, stirring occasionally, until the cabbage is tender and begins to caramelize about 10 mins.
5. Melt the remaining two tablespoons of butter in another skillet over medium heat. Add the boiled pierogi to the skillet in a single layer. Fry until they are golden and crispy on both sides, about 2-3 mins.
Per serving: Calories: 350 kcal, Protein: 8 g, Carbohydrates: 40 g, Fats: 18 g, Fiber: 4 g, Sodium:

Roasted Sausage and Grapes with Polenta

🕐 PREP: **15 mins** 🍳 COOK: **25 mins** 🍽 SERVES: **4**

Sausages: 1 pound (such as Italian sausage links)
Red Grapes: 1 cup, left whole.
Polenta: 1 cup dry (coarse cornmeal)
Chicken Broth: 4 cups (for cooking polenta)
Olive Oil: 2 tablespoons
Salt and Pepper: To taste

1. Preheat your oven to 425°F.
2. Place the sausages and whole grapes on a baking sheet. Drizzle with olive oil and season lightly with salt and pepper. Toss gently to coat. Arrange the sausages and grapes in a single layer to ensure even cooking.
3. Roast in the preheated oven for about 20-25 minutes, turning the sausages once halfway through, until the sausages are cooked through and the grapes are soft and slightly caramelized.
4. While the sausages and grapes are roasting, bring the chicken broth to a boil in a medium saucepan.
5. Gradually whisk in the polenta, reduce the heat to low, and cook, stirring frequently, until the polenta is thick and creamy, about 15-20 minutes. Season with salt to taste.
Per serving: Calories: 550 kcal, Protein: 20 g, Carbohydrates: 50 g, Fats: 30 g, Fiber: 2 g, Sodium: Moderate

Aleppo Pork Chops with Potatoes and Greens

🕐 PREP: **10 mins** 🔍 COOK: **30 mins** 🍽 SERVES: **4**

Pork Chops: 4 bone-in or boneless (about 6-8 ounces each)
Aleppo Pepper: 2 tablespoons (adjust based on spice preference)
Potatoes: 1 pound, cubed (small cubes for faster cooking)
Kale or Spinach: 2 cups, roughly chopped
Olive Oil: 3 tablespoons
Salt and Pepper: To taste

1. Preheat your oven to 425°F. This high heat will help to crisp the potatoes and sear the pork chops.
2. Toss the cubed potatoes with one tablespoon of olive oil, half the Aleppo pepper, and salt to taste. Spread them on a baking sheet in a single layer. Roast in the oven for about 20-25 minutes or until golden and crisp.
3. While the potatoes are roasting, season the pork chops with salt, pepper, and the remaining Aleppo pepper.
4. Heat 2 tablespoons of olive oil in a large skillet over medium-high heatAdd the pork chops and cook for about 4-5 minutes per side until they reach an internal temperature of 145°F (63°C) and are nicely browned.
5. Add the chopped kale or spinach to the same skillet used for the pork chops. Cook over medium heat, stirring occasionally, until the greens are wilted and tender, about 3-5 minutes—season with a salt.

Per serving: Calories: 450 kcal, Protein: 35 g, Carbohydrates: 25 g, Fats: 22 g, Fiber: 5 g, Sodium: Low

Keftedakia (Greek Meatballs)

🕐 PREP: **10 mins** 🔍 COOK: **15 mins** 🍽 SERVES: **4**

Ground Pork: 1 pound
Onion: 1 medium, finely grated
Garlic: 2 cloves, minced
Breadcrumbs: 1/2 cup
Egg: 1, beaten
Dried Oregano: 1 tablespoon
Salt and Pepper: To taste

1. Combine the ground pork, grated onion, minced garlic, breadcrumbs, beaten egg, dried oregano, salt, and pepper in a large mixing bowl.
2. Mix well until all ingredients are evenly distributed. It's best to use your hands to combine the mixture thoroughly.
3. Take small amounts of the meat mixture and roll it into balls about the size of a walnut or a golf ball. This size is traditional for Keftedakia, making them perfect for bite-sized eating.
4. Heat a few tablespoons of olive oil in a frying pan or skillet over medium heat.
5. Once the oil is hot, add the meatballs in batches, making sure not to overcrowd the pan. Fry the meatballs for about 8-10 minutes, turning them occasionally, until they are evenly browned on all sides and cooked through.
6. Once cooked, remove the meatballs from the skillet and place them on a plate lined with paper towels to drain any excess oil.

Per serving: Calories: 350 kcal, Protein: 24 g, Carbohydrates: 10 g, Fats: 22 g, Fiber: 1 g, Sodium: Low

Stuffed Courgettes with Egg and Lemon

⏰ PREP: **15 mins** 🔍 COOK: **25 mins** 🍽️ SERVES: **4**

Courgettes (Zucchini): 4 medium, halved lengthwise
Eggs: 2, beaten
Lemon Juice: 2 tablespoons
Rice: 1/2 cup, cooked (to help bind the filling)
Dill: 1 tablespoon, chopped
Salt and Pepper: To taste

1.Preheat your oven to 375°F (190°C).
2. Scoop out the flesh of the courgettes using a spoon or melon baller, leaving a shell about 1/4-inch thick. Chop the scooped-out flesh and set aside. Place the hollowed courgette halves in a baking dish and cut side up.
3. Combine the beaten eggs, lemon juice, cooked rice, chopped dill, and the reserved chopped courgette flesh in a mixing bowl—season with salt.
4. Mix well until all ingredients are thoroughly combined.
5. Spoon the egg and rice mixture into the hollowed courgette halves.
6. Cover the baking dish with aluminum foil and bake in the oven for about 20 minutes.
7. Remove the foil and bake for 5 minutes until the tops are slightly golden and the filling is set.
Per serving: Calories: 150 kcal, Protein: 6 g, Carbohydrates: 20 g, Fats: 5 g, Fiber: 3 g, Sodium: Low

Snails with Wheat Grains

⏰ PREP: **15 mins** 🔍 COOK: **1 hour** 🍽️ SERVES: **4**

Snails: 1 pound (fresh or canned; if fresh, ensure they are cleaned and purged)
Wheat Grains (Bulgur or Farro): 1 cup
Onion: 1 large, finely chopped
Garlic: 3 cloves, minced
Olive Oil: 2 tablespoons
Salt and Pepper: To taste

1. If fresh snails are used, they must be purged and cleaned first. Soak them in salted water for a few hours to remove impurities, then rinse thoroughly under cold water.
2. To cook thoroughly, boil the snails in fresh water for about 10-15 minutes. Drain and set aside.
3. In a large pot, bring 2 cups of water to a boil. Add the wheat grains, reduce the heat to a simmer, and cook covered until the grains are tender but still chewy, about 20-30 minutes for bulgur or 30-40 minutes for farro. Drain any excess water and set aside.
4. In a skillet, heat the olive oil over medium heat. Add the chopped onion and minced garlic. Sauté until the onion is translucent and the garlic is fragrant about 5-7 minutes.
5. Add the cooked snails to the skillet with the onions and garlic. Stir to combine.
6. Add the cooked wheat grains to the skillet. Mix well with the snails and onions. Cook together for 5-10 minutes, allowing flavors to meld—season with salt and pepper to taste.
Per serving: Calories: 550 kcal, Protein: 20 g, Carbohydrates: 50 g, Fats: 30 g, Fiber: 2 g, Sodium: Low

SEAFOOD

Squash Rice Paella with Mussels & Chorizo

⏰ PREP: **15 mins** ◎ COOK: **35 mins** 🍽 SERVES: **4**

Arborio Rice: 1 cup (or another short-grain rice suitable for paella)
Mussels: 1 pound, cleaned and debearded
Chorizo: 1/2 pound, sliced into rounds
Butternut Squash: 1 small, peeled and cubed
Chicken Stock: 3 cups
Saffron Threads: A pinch (for authentic flavor and color)

1. Heat the paella pan or a large skillet over medium heat. No oil is needed.
2. Add the sliced chorizo to the pan. Cook until it starts to crisp and releases its oils, about 5-7 minutes. Remove the chorizo and set aside.
3. In the chorizo oils, add the cubed butternut squash. Sauté it for about 10 minutes.
4. Stir in the Arborio rice and mix with the squash.
5. Warm the chicken stock in a separate pot and dissolve the saffron threads in it for a few minutes. Then, pour the saffron-infused stock over the rice.
6. Bring to a simmer, then reduce the heat to low. Cook without stirring for about 15 minutes.
7. When the rice is halfway cooked, tuck the mussels and cooked chorizo into the rice. Cover the pan with a lid or aluminum foil. Cook until the mussels have opened, about 10-15 mins.

Per serving: Calories: 550 kcal, Protein: 30 g, Carbohydrates: 60 g, Fats: 20 g, Fiber: 3 g

Spice Salmon

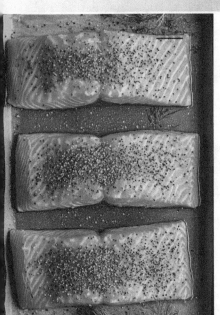

⏰ PREP: **15 mins** ◎ COOK: **15 mins** 🍽 SERVES: **4**

Salmon Fillets: 4 (about 6 ounces each)
Everything Bagel Seasoning: 4 tablespoons
Olive Oil: 2 tablespoons
Lemon Juice: 2 tablespoons (to finish before serving)
Salt: To taste (if your everything seasoning isn't already salted)
Fresh Dill: For garnish (optional)

1. Preheat your oven to 400°F.
2. Line a baking sheet with aluminum foil or parchment paper for easy cleanup.
3. Place the salmon fillets on the lined baking sheet.
Brush each fillet lightly with olive oil. This helps the seasoning to stick and enhances flavor.
4. Generously coat the top of each salmon fillet with everything bagel seasoning. If your seasoning blend doesn't include salt, lightly sprinkle each fillet with salt to taste.
5. Place the salmon in the oven and bake for about 12-15 minutes or until the fish flakes easily with a fork. The exact cooking time will depend on the thickness of the fillets.
6. Drizzle lemon juice over each fillet to add a bright, fresh flavor. Garnish with fresh dill if using.
Serve immediately, perhaps with roasted vegetables or a fresh salad.

Per serving: Calories: 300 kcal, Protein: 23 g, Carbohydrates: 1 g, Fats: 22 g, Fiber: 0 g, Sodium: Moderate

Clams in Salsa Verde with Sherry

⏰ PREP: **10 mins**   🎯 COOK: **15 mins**   🍽️ SERVES: **4**

Clams: 2 pounds, cleaned
Sherry: 1/2 cup (preferably a dry variety like Fino or Manzanilla)
Garlic: 3 cloves, minced
Parsley: 1/2 cup, finely chopped
Olive Oil: 2 tablespoons
Salt and Pepper: To taste

1. Combine the finely chopped parsley, minced garlic, olive oil, and a pinch of salt and pepper in a small bowl. Mix well to create the salsa verde.
2. Heat a large pot or skillet over medium heat. Add the salsa verde and cook for 1-2 minutes until the garlic becomes fragrant, stirring frequently to prevent burning.
3. Pour in the sherry and bring the mixture to a simmer. Add the clams to the pot, stirring them into the sauce.
4. Cover the pot with a lid and cook for 5-7 minutes or until the clams have opened. Discard any clams that do not open.
5. Once the clams are cooked, gently shake or stir the pot to coat the clams evenly in the salsa verde.

Per serving: Calories: 200 kcal, Protein: 14 g, Carbohydrates: 8 g, Fats: 10 g, Fiber: 0 g, Sodium: High

Grilled Oysters with Fennel and Sage

⏰ PREP: **10 mins**   🎯 COOK: **10 mins**   🍽️ SERVES: **4**

Oysters: 24 fresh oysters, shucked (keep half shell for grilling)
Fennel Bulb: 1 small, finely chopped
Sage: 1 tablespoon, freshly chopped
Butter: 4 tablespoons, melted.
Lemon Juice: 2 tablespoons
Salt and Pepper: To taste

1. Preheat your grill to medium-high heat.
2. Combine the melted butter, finely chopped fennel, chopped sage, lemon juice, and a pinch of salt and pepper in a small bowl. Stir well to mix.
3. Arrange the shucked oysters on their half shells on a tray. Make sure to retain some of their natural liquor in the shell, which helps to steam them while grilling.
4. Brush a generous amount of the fennel and sage butter mixture over each oyster. The herbs and butter will help to flavor the oysters as they grill.
5. Place the oysters (on their half shells) directly on the grill. Grill for about 4-7 minutes, or until the edges of the oysters begin to curl and the butter is bubbling.
6. Remove the oysters from the grill carefully using tongs. Arrange them on a serving platter.

Per serving: Calories: 210 kcal, Protein: 10 g, Carbohydrates: 5 g, Fats: 16 g, Fiber: 1 g, Sodium: Moderate

Spicy Olive Oil-Poached Shrimp

⏰ PREP: **15 mins** 🔍 COOK: **10 mins** 🍽 SERVES: **4**

Shrimp: 1 pound, peeled and deveined (large or jumbo size)
Olive Oil: 1 cup (enough to cover the shrimp in a small pot)
Garlic: 3 cloves, thinly sliced
Red Pepper Flakes: 1 teaspoon (adjust based on heat preference)
Lemon Zest: From 1 lemon
Salt: To taste

1. Rinse the shrimp under cold water and pat dry with paper towels. Prepare garlic slices and lemon zest.
2. Pour the olive oil into a small pot or saucepan. Add the thinly sliced garlic and red pepper flakes.
3. Heat the oil over low heat until warm but not simmering (about 135-140°F or 57-60°C). The goal is to gently infuse the oil without frying the garlic.
4. Add the shrimp to the warm oil. Ensure they are submerged.
Poach the shrimp in the oil until they are pink and opaque, about 5-7 minutes, depending on their size. Be careful not to overcook.
5. Transfer the shrimp to a bowl or serving dish using a slotted spoon.
Season with salt and sprinkle over the lemon zest for a fresh, citrusy note. Spoon some infused oil over the shrimp, including the garlic and red pepper flakes.
Per serving: Calories: 300 kcal, Protein: 24 g, Carbohydrates: 1 g, Fats: 22 g, Fiber: 0 g, Sodium: Low

Grilled Branzino with Peperonata

⏰ PREP: **15 mins** 🔍 COOK: **25 mins** 🍽 SERVES: **4**

Branzino: 2 whole fish, gutted and scaled (about 1 to 1.5 pounds each)
Red Bell Peppers: 2 large, sliced
Yellow Bell Peppers: 2 large, sliced
Olive Oil: 4 tablespoons (divided for grilling and sautéing)
Garlic: 3 cloves, minced
Salt and Pepper: To taste

1. Heat 2 tablespoons of olive oil in a large skillet over medium heat.
2. Add the sliced red and yellow bell peppers and minced garlic. Sauté until the peppers are soft and lightly caramelized, about 15-20 minutes.
3. Season with salt and pepper to taste. Reduce heat to low and keep warm while you grill the branzino.
4. Rinse the branzino under cold water and pat dry with paper towels. Make several diagonal slashes on each side of the fish to help the heat penetrate more evenly during grilling.
5. Brush the fish with the remaining two tablespoons of olive oil and season inside and out with salt and pepper.
6. Preheat your grill or grill pan to medium-high heat. Place the branzino on the grill and cook for about 6-7 minutes per side, or until the skin is crisp and the flesh is opaque and flakes easily with a fork.
Per serving: Calories: 350 kcal, Protein: 44 g, Carbohydrates: 12 g, Fats: 16 g, Fiber: 3 g, Sodium: Moderate

Easy Carbonara with Scallops and Peas

⏰ PREP: **15 mins** ◎ COOK: **20 mins** 🍴🍽 SERVES: **4**

Spaghetti: 1 pound
Scallops: 1 pound, patted dry.
Frozen Peas: 1 cup
Eggs: 2 large
Parmesan Cheese: 1 cup, grated
Garlic: 2 cloves, minced

1. Bring a large pot of salted water to a boil.
2. Cook spaghetti according to package instructions until al dente. Reserve 1 cup of water for later use, then drain the pasta.
3. In a mixing bowl, whisk together the eggs and grated Parmesan cheese.
4. Heat a large skillet over medium-high heat. Add a splash of olive oil and the minced garlic. Sauté for about 1 minute until fragrant.
5. Add the scallops to the skillet. Cook for 2-3 minutes on each side or until golden brown and cooked through. Remove the scallops and set aside.
6. In the same skillet, add the frozen peas and cook for 2-3 minutes.
7. Reduce the heat to low and add the cooked spaghetti to the skillet.
8. Quickly pour the egg and cheese mixture over the pasta, tossing continuously with tongs to coat the pasta without cooking the eggs thoroughly. Add a little of the reserved pasta water to achieve a creamy consistency. Return the scallops to the skillet and toss gently to combine.

Per serving: Calories: 650 kcal, Protein: 45 g, Carbohydrates: 85 g, Fats: 15 g, Fiber: 4 g, Sodium: Low

Crab Salad with Tangy Pickle Dressing

⏰ PREP: **15 mins** ◎ COOK: **15 mins** 🍽 SERVES: **4**

Crab Meat: 1 pound, cooked and shredded or chunked
Mixed Salad Greens: 4 cups (such as arugula, spinach, and romaine)
Dill Pickles: 1/2 cup, finely chopped
Olive Oil: 3 tablespoons
Lemon Juice: 2 tablespoons
Salt and Pepper: To taste

1. Combine the finely chopped dill pickles, olive oil, and lemon juice in a small bowl or jar. Whisk or shake vigorously to blend—season with salt and pepper to taste.
2. In a large mixing bowl, place the mixed salad greens. Add the cooked crab meat to the greens.
3. Pour the tangy pickle dressing over the salad and crab meat. Gently toss everything together until well coated with the dressing.
4. Divide the salad among plates or bowls.
5. Optionally, garnish with additional pickle slices, fresh dill, or a sprinkle of lemon zest for extra flavor and visual appeal.

Per serving: Calories: 230 kcal, Protein: 24 g, Carbohydrates: 4 g, Fats: 14 g, Fiber: 1 g, Sodium: Moderate

Garlic Shrimp Spaghetti with Buttery Kale

⏰ PREP: **10 mins** 🔍 COOK: **20 mins** 🍽️ SERVES: **4**

Spaghetti: 1 pound
Shrimp: 1 pound, peeled and deveined
Garlic: 4 cloves, minced
Kale: 2 cups, chopped
Butter: 4 tablespoons
Salt and Pepper: To taste

1. Bring a large pot of salted water to a boil. Add the spaghetti and cook according to package instructions until al dente. Reserve 1 cup of pasta water for later use, drain the spaghetti, and set aside.
2. While the pasta is cooking, heat two tablespoons of butter in a skillet.
3. Add the minced garlic to the skillet and sauté for about 1 minute.
4. Add the shrimp to the skillet—season with salt and pepper. Cook for 2-3 minutes per side or until the shrimp are pink and opaque. Remove the shrimp from the skillet and set aside.
5. In the same skillet, add the remaining two tablespoons of butter. Add the chopped kale and sauté until the kale begins to wilt and tender, about 5 minutes. Return the cooked shrimp to the skillet with the kale. Add the drained spaghetti to the skillet. Toss everything together, adding more reserved pasta water to loosen the sauce and coat the spaghetti.

Per serving: Calories: 500 kcal, Protein: 35 g, Carbohydrates: 70 g, Fats: 12 g, Fiber: 3 g, Sodium: Moderate

Fennel-Crusted Side of Salmon with Yogurt Sauce

⏰ PREP: **15 mins** 🔍 COOK: **20 mins** 🍽️ SERVES: **4**

Salmon: 1 large side of salmon, skin on (about 2 pounds)
Fennel Seeds: 2 tablespoons, coarsely crushed
Yogurt: 1 cup, plain (Greek yogurt for a thicker consistency)
Chives: 2 tablespoons, finely chopped
Lemon Juice: 1 tablespoon
Salt and Pepper: To taste

1. Preheat your oven to 400°F (200°C).
2. Rinse the salmon under cold water and pat dry with paper towels.
3. Place the salmon, skin side down, on a lightly greased baking sheet.
4. Rub the top of the salmon with crushed fennel seeds and season generously with salt and pepper.
5. Place the salmon in the oven and bake for 15-20 minutes, or until the salmon is cooked through and flakes easily with a fork. The cooking time may vary depending on the thickness of the salmon.
6. While the salmon is baking, prepare the sauce. Combine the yogurt, chopped chives, and lemon juice in a small bowl. Mix well until smooth.
7. Season the sauce with salt and pepper to taste.

Per serving: Calories: 350 kcal, Protein: 34 g, Carbohydrates: 4 g, Fats: 20 g, Fiber: 1 g, Sodium: Low

Fish Taco Lettuce Wraps

⏰ PREP: **10 mins** 🎯 COOK: **10 mins** 🍽 SERVES: **4**

White Fish Fillets: 1 pound (like tilapia, cod, or halibut)
Lime: 2 (juice for marinating and extra wedges for serving)
Garlic Powder: 1 teaspoon
Avocado: 1, sliced
Lettuce Leaves: 8 large leaves (such as butter lettuce, iceberg, or romaine for wrapping)
Pico de Gallo: 1 cup (homemade or store-bought)

1. In a mixing bowl, squeeze the juice of one lime over the fish fillets. Sprinkle with garlic powder and a pinch of salt. Let marinate for about 5 minutes while you prepare the other ingredients.
2. Heat a non-stick skillet over medium heat. Add the marinated fish to the skillet and cook for about 4-5 minutes per side, or until it is opaque and flakes easily with a fork. Remove from heat and break into large chunks.
3. Wash the lettuce leaves and pat dry. Choose leaves that can hold the filling like little cups. Slice the avocado and set aside.
4. Place a lettuce leaf on a plate. Add a scoop of the cooked fish, a few slices of avocado, and a generous spoonful of pico de gallo.

Per serving: Calories: 200 kcal, Protein: 23 g, Carbohydrates: 9 g, Fats: 8 g, Fiber: 3 g, Sodium: Low

Roasted Grape and Salmon Kale Salad

⏰ PREP: **10 mins** 🎯 COOK: **20 mins** 🍽 SERVES: **4**

Salmon Fillets: 4 (about 6 ounces each)
Red Grapes: 1 cup, halved
Kale: 4 cups, roughly chopped and stems removed
Olive Oil: 2 tablespoons (plus extra for drizzling on salmon and grapes)
Lemon Juice: 2 tablespoons
Salt and Pepper: To taste

1. Preheat your oven to 400°F (200°C).
2. Place the salmon fillets on one half of a baking sheet and the halved grapes on the other half.
3. Drizzle the salmon and grapes with olive oil and season with salt.
4. Roast in the preheated oven for about 15-20 minutes, or until the salmon is cooked and flakes easily, and the grapes are juicy and slightly caramelized.
5. While the salmon and grapes are roasting, place the chopped kale in a large mixing bowl.
6. Drizzle with olive oil and lemon juice, and season with salt. Massage the kale with your hands for about 2-3 minutes until the leaves soften and wilt slightly. This process makes the kale more tender and palatable.
7. Once the salmon and grapes are done, let them cool slightly. Flake the salmon into large chunks. Add the roasted grapes and flaked salmon to the bowl of kale.
8. Toss everything gently to combine. Transfer to a salad bowl or platter and serve immediately.

Per serving: Calories: 350 kcal, Protein: 25 g, Carbohydrates: 15 g, Fats: 20 g, Fiber: 2 g, Sodium: Low

Roasted Cod and Potatoes with Chorizo Vinaigrette

🕐 PREP: **15 mins** 🔍 COOK: **30 mins** 🍽️ SERVES: **4**

Cod Fillets: 4 (about 6 ounces each)
Baby Potatoes: 1 pound, halved or quartered depending on size
Chorizo: 4 ounces, diced
Olive Oil: 2 tablespoons
Red Wine Vinegar: 2 tablespoons
Parsley: 2 tablespoons, chopped (for garnish)

1. Preheat your oven to 425°F (220°C).
2. Toss the halved baby potatoes with one tablespoon of olive oil.
3. Spread the potatoes on a baking sheet in a single layer.
Roast in the oven for about 20 minutes or until they become tender.
4. After the potatoes roast for 20 minutes, make space on the baking sheet and add the cod fillets.
5. Drizzle the cod with the remaining tablespoon of olive oil.
6. Return the baking sheet to the oven and roast the cod and potatoes together for 10-12 minutes, or until the cod is opaque and flakes easily.
7. Heat a small skillet over medium heat while the cod and potatoes roast.
8. Add the diced chorizo and cook until it releases its oils and becomes slightly crispy about 3-4 minutes.
Per serving: Calories: 350 kcal, Protein: 26 g, Carbohydrates: 22 g, Fats: 18 g, Fiber: 3 g, Sodium: Low

Cod in Parchment with Orange-Leek Couscous

🕐 PREP: **15 mins** 🔍 COOK: **20 mins** 🍽️ SERVES: **4**

Cod Fillets: 4 (about 6 ounces each)
Couscous: 1 cup
Leeks: 1 large, thinly sliced
Orange Zest: From 1 orange
Olive Oil: 2 tablespoons
Salt and Pepper: To taste

1. Preheat your oven to 400°F.
2. Bring 1 1/2 cups of water to a boil in a pot. Add the couscous, half of the orange zest, and a pinch of salt. Stir, cover, and remove from heat.
3. Let the couscous sit for 5 minutes, then fluff with a fork. Mix in the thinly sliced leeks.
4. Cut four large pieces of parchment paper (about 15 inches long each).
5. Divide the couscous mixture among the four pieces of parchment, placing it in the center.
6. Place a cod fillet on top of each bed of couscous. Drizzle with olive oil and season with salt, pepper, and orange zest.
7. Fold the parchment over the cod and couscous, twisting the ends to seal each packet.
8. Place the parchment packets on a baking sheet. Bake in the oven for 15-20 minutes or until the cod is opaque and flakes easily with a fork.
Per serving: Calories: 350 kcal, Protein: 28 g, Carbohydrates: 33 g, Fats: 10 g, Fiber: 3 g, Sodium: Low

Bucatini with Tuna and Bread Crumbs

⏰ PREP: **5 mins** 🍳 COOK: **15 mins** 🍽️ SERVES: **4**

Bucatini Pasta: 1 pound
Canned Tuna: 2 cans (about 5 ounces each), drained.
Bread Crumbs: 1/2 cup, ideally homemade for better texture
Garlic: 2 cloves, minced
Olive Oil: 4 tablespoons
Parsley: 1/4 cup, chopped (for garnish and added flavor)

1. Bring a large pot of salted water to a boil.
2. Add the bucatini pasta and cook according to package instructions.
3. Reserve 1 cup of cooking water, drain the pasta, and set aside.
4. Heat 2 tablespoons of olive oil over medium heat in a large skillet.
5. Add the minced garlic and sauté until fragrant, about 1 minute.
6. Add the bread crumbs to the skillet and toast them, stirring frequently, until golden and crispy, about 3-5 minutes. 7. In the same skillet, add the remaining two tablespoons of olive oil.
7. Add the drained tuna and break it up slightly with a fork.
8. Add the cooked pasta to the skillet with the tuna. Toss well to combine, adding a bit of the reserved pasta water to moisten the mixture.
9. Divide the pasta among plates. Sprinkle the toasted bread crumbs and chopped parsley over the top of the pasta. Serve immediately, offering additional olive oil or lemon wedges if desired.

Per serving: Calories: 600 kcal, Protein: 25 g, Carbohydrates: 85 g, Fats: 18 g, Fiber: 4 g, Sodium: Low

Crusted Seared Swordfish with Olive Gremolata

⏰ PREP: **10 mins** 🍳 COOK: **10 mins** 🍽️ SERVES: **4**

Swordfish Steaks: 4 (about 6 ounces each, 1 inch thick)
Breadcrumbs: 1/2 cup, preferably panko, for a crispier crust
Green Olives: 1/2 cup, finely chopped
Parsley: 1/4 cup, finely chopped
Lemon Zest: From 1 lemon
Olive Oil: 4 tablespoons, divided

1. Combine the finely chopped green olives, chopped parsley, and lemon zest in a small bowl. Mix well to blend the flavors. Set aside for garnishing the fish.
2. Pat the swordfish steaks dry with paper towels. Season both sides of the steaks with salt and pepper (not included in the ingredient count, as they are pantry staples).
3. Press the breadcrumbs onto one side of each steak to form a crust.
4. Heat 2 tablespoons of olive oil in a large skillet over medium-high heat. Once the oil is hot, add the swordfish steaks, crusted side down, and sear for about 4-5 minutes until the breadcrumbs are golden and crispy.
5. Carefully flip the steaks, add the remaining two tablespoons of olive oil, and cook for another 4-5 minutes or until the fish reaches an internal temperature of 145°F and is opaque.

Per serving: Calories: 350 kcal, Protein: 35 g, Carbohydrates: 10 g, Fats: 18 g, Fiber: 1 g, Sodium: Low

Tuna Friselle

🕐 PREP: **10 mins** ◎ COOK: **10 mins** 🍽 SERVES: **4**

Friselle: 4 (traditional twice-baked Italian bread rings)
Canned Tuna: 1 can (about 5 ounces), drained and flaked
Cherry Tomatoes: 1 cup, halved
Olive Oil: 2 tablespoons
Red Onion: 1/4 cup, finely sliced
Salt and Pepper: To taste

1. Briefly soak the friselle in water to slightly soften them, but they should remain somewhat crunchy. This should take a maximum of a few seconds so they don't become too soggy.
2. Combine the flaked tuna, cherry tomatoes, sliced red onion, and olive oil in a mixing bowl—season with salt and pepper.
3. Top each softened friselle with an even portion of the tuna mixture.
4. Serve immediately, ensuring the friselle retains some of its crunch for textural contrast.

Per serving: Calories: 250-300 kcal, Protein: 15-20 g, Carbohydrates: 20-25 g, Fats: 10-15 g, Fiber: 2-3 g, Sodium: Low

Cuttlefish with Spinach

🕐 PREP: **10 mins** ◎ COOK: **20 mins** 🍽 SERVES: **4**

Cuttlefish: 1 pound, cleaned and cut into strips or rings
Spinach: 1 pound, fresh and washed
Garlic: 2 cloves, minced
Olive Oil: 2 tablespoons
Lemon Juice: 1 tablespoon
Salt and Pepper: To taste

1. If the cuttlefish hasn't been cleaned, remove the ink sac, cuttlebone, and internal organs. Rinse under cold water and pat dry.
2. Heat one tablespoon of olive oil in a large pot over medium heat.
3. Add half of the minced garlic and sauté for about 30 seconds until fragrant.
4. Gradually add the spinach to the pot, stirring until it wilts down. This may need to be done in batches, depending on the size of your pot. Once the spinach is wilted and heated through, season with salt and pepper. Transfer to a serving platter and keep warm.
5. In the same skillet, heat the remaining olive oil over medium-high heat.
6. Add the remaining garlic and sauté for about 30 seconds until fragrant.
7. Add the cuttlefish and sauté for about 5-7 minutes, or until the cuttlefish is opaque and cooked through. 8. Be careful not to overcook as it can become rubbery. Sprinkle with lemon juice, and season with salt and pepper to taste.

Per serving: Calories: 180 kcal, Protein: 25 g, Carbohydrates: 5 g, Fats: 7 g, Fiber: 2 g, Sodium: Low

VEGETABLE,

VEGETARIAN

&

GRAIN DISHES

One-Pot Spaghetti Puttanesca

⏰ PREP: **15 mins**   🔍 COOK: **20 mins**   🍽️ SERVES: **4**

Spaghetti: 1 pound
Canned Tomatoes: 1 can (28 ounces), crushed
Anchovy Fillets: 6, chopped (they dissolve and add a rich, salty flavor)
Capers: 2 tablespoons, rinsed
Black Olives: 1/2 cup, pitted and chopped
Garlic: 4 cloves, minced

1. Combine the uncooked spaghetti, diced tomatoes (with their juice), anchovies, minced garlic, olives, capers, red pepper flakes, and olive oil in a large, deep skillet or a heavy-bottomed pot. Spread the ingredients evenly and lay the spaghetti flat.
2. Pour in the water and bring the mixture to a boil over high heat. Use tongs to toss everything as the water starts to boil.
3. Reduce the heat to a medium simmer. Continue cooking, stirring frequently, for about 10-12 minutes or until the pasta is al dente and most of the liquid has been absorbed by the pasta or evaporated. The ingredients will meld together during this time and create a flavorful sauce.
4. Once the pasta is cooked and the sauce has thickened, remove it from heat and season with salt and black pepper to taste.

Per Serving: Calories: 300 kcal, Protein: 8 g, Carbohydrates: 40 g, Fats: 12 g, Fiber: 5 g, Sodium: Low

Roasted Cauliflower and Chickpea Bowl

⏰ PREP: **15 mins**   🔍 COOK: **20 mins**   🍽️ SERVES: **4**

Cauliflower: 1 large head, cut into florets.
Chickpeas: 1 can (15 ounces), drained and rinsed
Olive Oil: 2 tablespoons
Paprika: 1 teaspoon
Garlic Powder: 1 teaspoon
Salt and Pepper: To taste

1. Preheat your oven to 425°F (220°C).
2. In a large mixing bowl, combine the cauliflower florets and drained chickpeas.
3. Drizzle with olive oil and sprinkle with paprika, garlic powder, salt, and pepper. Toss everything together until well coated.
4. Spread the cauliflower and chickpeas in a single layer on a baking sheet.
5. Roast in the preheated oven for about 25 minutes, or until the cauliflower is tender and the edges are golden brown, stirring halfway through for even cooking.
6. Remove from the oven and let cool slightly. Serve the roasted cauliflower and chickpeas warm as a standalone bowl or over a bed of greens, quinoa, or rice for a more filling meal.

Per serving: Calories: 250 kcal, Protein: 9 g, Carbohydrates: 27 g, Fats: 12 g, Fiber: 8 g, Sodium: Low

Lemon Tahini Smothered Broccolini with Seeds

⏰ PREP: **5 mins** 🔍 COOK: **15 mins** 🍽️ SERVES: **4**

Broccolini: 1 pound, ends trimmed
Tahini: 1/4 cup
Lemon Juice: 2 tablespoons
Mixed Seeds (such as sunflower, sesame, and pumpkin seeds):
1/4 cup, toasted
Garlic: 1 clove, minced
Salt and Pepper: To taste

1. Bring a pot of water to a boil and blanch the broccolini for about 2 minutes until bright green and tender. Alternatively, steam in a steamer basket over boiling water for 3-4 minutes. Drain well.
2. Whisk together tahini, lemon juice, minced garlic, and enough water (about two tablespoons) in a small bowl to achieve a pourable consistency—season with salt and pepper to taste.
3. Heat a small pan over medium heat. Add the mixed seeds and toast, stirring frequently, until golden and fragrant. Be careful not to burn them.
4. Arrange the steamed or blanched broccolini on a serving platter. Drizzle the lemon tahini sauce generously over the broccolini. Sprinkle the toasted seeds over the top.

Per serving: Calories: 180 kcal, Protein: 6 g, Carbohydrates: 12 g, Fats: 13 g, Fiber: 3 g, Sodium: Moderate

Grilled Veggie Flatbread

⏰ PREP: **15 mins** 🔍 COOK: **15 mins** 🍽️ SERVES: **4**

Flatbread or Naan: 4 pieces
Zucchini: 1 medium, sliced
Bell Pepper: 1 large, sliced (choose any color)
Red Onion: 1 medium, sliced
Olive Oil: 2 tablespoons for brushing and grilling
Salt and Pepper: To taste

1. Preheat your grill to medium-high heat.
2. Toss the sliced zucchini, bell pepper, and red onion with olive oil, salt, and pepper until evenly coated.
3. Place the vegetables on the grill and cook for 2-3 minutes on each side, or until they have excellent, tender grill marks. Remove from the grill and set aside.
4. Brush each flatbread lightly with olive oil.
Place the flatbread on the grill for about 1-2 minutes on each side until warm and slightly crispy.
5. Arrange the grilled vegetables evenly over the warmed flatbread.
6. If desired, sprinkle crumbled feta cheese and fresh herbs over the top before serving. Cut into pieces and serve immediately while still warm.

Per serving: Calories: 300 kcal, Protein: 8 g, Carbohydrates: 40 g, Fats: 12 g, Fiber: 5 g, Sodium: Low

Butternut Noodles Cacio e Pepe

🕐 PREP: **10 mins**   🔍 COOK: **15 mins**   🍽 SERVES: **4**

Butternut Squash Noodles: 4 cups (pre-spiralized, or you can spiralize a medium butternut squash)
Pecorino Romano Cheese: 1 cup, finely grated
Black Pepper: 2 teaspoons, freshly cracked
Butter: 2 tablespoons
Olive Oil: 1 tablespoon

1. If using a whole butternut squash, peel it and use a spiralizer to create noodles. If pre-spiralized, ensure they are ready to cook.
2. Heat the olive oil and butter in a large skillet over medium heat.
3. Add the butternut noodles to the skillet, season with a pinch of salt, and sauté for about 5-7 minutes, or until the noodles are tender but still hold their shape.
4. Reduce the heat to low. Add the freshly cracked black pepper to the noodles and toss well to distribute.
5. Gradually add the grated Pecorino Romano cheese while tossing the noodles with tongs. If the noodles seem dry, add a small splash of water or more olive oil to help the cheese melt and coat the noodles evenly.

Per serving: Calories: 250 kcal, Protein: 8 g, Carbohydrates: 20 g, Fats: 16 g, Fiber: 3 g, Sodium: Moderate

Creamy Kale Pasta

🕐 PREP: **10 mins**   🔍 COOK: **10 mins**   🍽 SERVES: **4**

Kale: 2 cups, stems removed and leaves chopped
Cashews: 1/2 cup, soaked for at least 4 hours or overnight if not using a high-powered blender
Garlic: 2 cloves
Lemon Juice: 2 tablespoons
Olive Oil: 1/4 cup
Salt: 1/2 teaspoon, or to taste

1. If you prefer a milder kale flavor, blanch the Kale leaves briefly in boiling water for 1-2 minutes, then rinse under cold water and drain well. This step also helps to soften the Kale and bring out a vibrant green color.
2. Combine the blanched or raw Kale, soaked and drained cashews, garlic, lemon juice, olive oil, and salt in a food processor or blender.
Blend until the mixture is completely smooth. If the paste is too thick, add some water or olive oil to reach your desired consistency.
3. Taste the kale paste and adjust the seasoning with more salt or lemon juice if needed.

Per serving: Calories: 150 kcal, Protein: 3 g, Carbohydrates: 8 g, Fats: 12 g, Fiber: 1 g, Sodium: Low

Black Bean Stuffed Poblano Peppers

🕐 PREP: **15 mins** 🔍 COOK: **15 mins** 🍽 SERVES: **4**

Poblano Peppers: 4 large, halved and seeded
Black Beans: 1 can (15 ounces), rinsed and drained
Corn: 1 cup, frozen and thawed or fresh
Cheddar Cheese: 1 cup shredded
Cumin: 1 teaspoon
Salt and Pepper: To taste

1. Preheat your oven to 375°F (190°C).
2. Halve the poblano peppers lengthwise and remove the seeds and membranes. Arrange the pepper halves on a baking sheet and cut side up.
3. Combine the rinsed black beans, corn, half of the shredded cheddar cheese, cumin, salt, and pepper in a mixing bowl. Mix well to ensure the flavors are evenly distributed.
4. Spoon the black bean mixture evenly into each poblano pepper half. Sprinkle the remaining cheddar cheese over the top of the stuffed peppers.
5. Place the baking sheet in the oven and bake for about 20 minutes until the peppers are tender and the cheese is melted and bubbly.

Per serving: Calories: 250 kcal, Protein: 12 g, Carbohydrates: 28 g, Fats: 10 g, Fiber: 7 g, Sodium: Moderate

Summer Squash, Mint, and Pecorino Pasta

🕐 PREP: **10 mins** 🔍 COOK: **10 mins** 🍽 SERVES: **4**

Pasta: 1 pound (such as spaghetti or linguine)
Summer Squash: 2 medium, thinly sliced
Fresh Mint: 1/4 cup, chopped
Pecorino Cheese: 1/2 cup, freshly grated
Olive Oil: 2 tablespoons
Salt and Pepper: To taste

1. Bring a large pot of salted water to a boil. Cook the pasta according to package instructions until al dente. Reserve 1 cup of pasta water, drain the pasta and set aside.
2. While the pasta is cooking, heat the olive oil in a large skillet over medium heat.
3. Add the sliced summer squash and sauté until tender and slightly golden, about 5-7 minutes.
4. Season with salt and pepper to taste.
5. Add the cooked pasta to the skillet with the summer squash. If the mixture seems dry, add some reserved pasta water to help loosen it up. Stir in the chopped fresh mint and half of the grated Pecorino cheese. Toss everything together until well combined, and the cheese starts to melt.

Per serving: Calories: 450 kcal, Protein: 18 g, Carbohydrates: 65 g, Fats: 15 g, Fiber: 3 g, Sodium: Low

Spicy Lentils with Tomato

⏰ PREP: **15 mins** ◉ COOK: **25 mins** 🍽 SERVES: **4**

Lentils: 1 cup, dry (prefer brown or green lentils for their texture)
Canned Tomatoes: 1 can (14 ounces), diced
Onion: 1 large, diced
Garlic: 2 cloves, minced
Red Chili Flakes: 1 teaspoon (adjust to taste)
Olive Oil: 2 tablespoons

1. Rinse the lentils under cold running water. In a pot, add the lentils and cover with water (about 2 inches above the lentils).
2. Bring to a boil, then reduce heat and simmer for 20-25 minutes or until the lentils are tender but still hold their shape. Drain any excess water.
3. While the lentils are cooking, heat the olive oil in a sauté pan over medium heat. Add the diced onion and minced garlic. Cook until the onion is translucent and the garlic is fragrant about 5 minutes.
4. Add the canned tomatoes (with their juices) and red chili flakes to the onion and garlic mixture. Stir to combine. Add the cooked and drained lentils to the pan. Stir well to integrate all the flavors. Season with salt and pepper to taste.
5. Let the mixture simmer for 5-10 minutes to allow the flavors to meld.
Per serving: Calories: 270 kcal, Protein: 14 g, Carbohydrates: 38 g, Fats: 7 g, Fiber: 16 g, Sodium: Low

Lentils with Saffron

⏰ PREP: **5 mins** ◉ COOK: **25 mins** 🍽 SERVES: **4**

Lentils: 1 cup, dry (choose a variety like green or Puy for best texture)
Saffron Threads: A generous pinch
Onion: 1 medium, finely chopped
Garlic: 2 cloves, minced
Vegetable Stock: 2 cups (or water)
Olive Oil: 2 tablespoons
Salt and Pepper: To taste

1. In a small bowl, throw the saffron threads in two tablespoons of hot water. This will help release their color and fragrance.
2. Rinse the lentils under cold water until the water runs clear. Combine the lentils with the vegetable stock (or water) in a pot. Bring to a boil, then reduce heat and simmer for about 20-25 minutes or until the lentils are tender but not mushy. Drain any excess liquid.
3. While the lentils are cooking, heat the olive oil in a skillet over medium heat.
4. Add the chopped onion and minced garlic. Sauté until the onion is translucent and the garlic is aromatic, about 5 minutes.
5. Once the lentils are cooked, add them to the skillet with the onions and garlic. Pour the saffron and its soaking liquid into the skillet. Stir well to distribute the saffron evenly. Cook together for a few minutes to allow the flavors to meld. Season with salt and pepper to taste.
Per serving: Calories: 230 kcal, Protein: 14 g, Carbohydrates: 32 g, Fats: 5 g, Fiber: 16 g, Sodium: Low

Green Beans with Tomato

⏰ PREP: **10 mins** 🔍 COOK: **15 mins** 🍽 SERVES: **4**

Green Beans: 1 pound, trimmed
Cherry Tomatoes: 1 pint, halved
Garlic: 3 cloves, minced
Olive Oil: 2 tablespoons
Basil: A few leaves, chopped (or one teaspoon dried)
Salt and Pepper: To taste

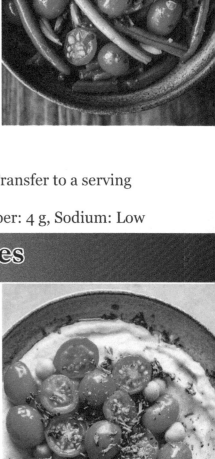

1. Bring a large pot of salted water to a boil. Add the green beans and blanch for 2-3 minutes until they are bright green and tender.
2. Drain the beans and immediately rinse under cold water to stop cooking.
3. Heat the olive oil in a large skillet over medium heat. Add the minced garlic and sauté for about 1 minute until fragrant.
4. Add the blanched green beans to the skillet. Toss them in the garlic and olive oil.
5. Cook for about 2 minutes, then add the halved cherry tomatoes. Continue to cook for another 5-7 minutes, stirring occasionally, until the tomatoes break down and the green beans are tender but still crisp.
6. Season the green beans and tomatoes with salt and pepper to taste.
7. Stir in the chopped basil just before removing it from the heat for freshness. Transfer to a serving dish and serve warm or at room temperature.

Per serving: Calories: 120 kcal, Protein: 2 g, Carbohydrates: 10 g, Fats: 8 g, Fiber: 4 g, Sodium: Low

Chickpea Puree with Tomatoes

⏰ PREP: **10 mins** 🔍 COOK: **15 mins** 🍽 SERVES: **4**

Chickpeas: 1 can (15 ounces), drained and rinsed
Cherry Tomatoes: 1 cup, halved
Garlic: 1 clove
Olive Oil: 2 tablespoons
Lemon Juice: 1 tablespoon
Salt and Pepper: To taste

1. If using canned chickpeas, rinse them thoroughly under cold water to remove the canning liquid, which can be high in sodium and have a tinny taste.
2. Combine the drained chickpeas, garlic, olive oil, and lemon juice in a food processor or blender.
3. Blend until smooth. If the mixture is too thick, add a little water or olive oil to achieve a creamy consistency. Season with salt and pepper to taste.
4. Toss the halved cherry tomatoes in a small bowl with olive oil and a pinch of salt.

Per serving: Calories: 220 kcal, Protein: 7 g, Carbohydrates: 23 g, Fats: 11 g, Fiber: 6 g, Sodium: Low

Beans with Tomato

⏰ PREP: **5 mins** ◎ COOK: **20 mins** 🍽 SERVES: **4**

Beans: 2 cans (15 ounces each), such as cannellini or kidney beans, drained and rinsed
Canned Tomatoes: 1 can (14 ounces), diced
Onion: 1 medium, chopped
Garlic: 2 cloves, minced
Olive Oil: 2 tablespoons
Salt and Pepper: To taste

1. Heat the olive oil in a large skillet or saucepan over medium heat. Add the chopped onion and minced garlic. Cook, stirring frequently, until the onion becomes translucent and the garlic is fragrant about 3-4 minutes.
2. Stir in the canned tomatoes (with their juices). Bring a simmer and cook for 5 minutes to let the flavors meld.
3. Add the drained and rinsed beans to the skillet. Stir to combine with the tomato and onion mixture.
4. Reduce heat to low and simmer for another 10-15 minutes, allowing the beans to absorb the flavors and the sauce to thicken slightly.

Per serving: Calories: 260 kcal, Protein: 12 g, Carbohydrates: 38 g, Fats: 7 g, Fiber: 10 g, Sodium: Moderate

Creamed Beans with Carrots

⏰ PREP: **10 mins** ◎ COOK: **15 mins** 🍽 SERVES: **4**

White Beans: 1 can (15 ounces), such as cannellini or navy beans, drained and rinsed
Carrots: 2 large, peeled and finely diced
Heavy Cream: 1/2 cup
Butter: 2 tablespoons
Garlic: 2 cloves, minced
Salt and Pepper: To taste

1. In a skillet, melt the butter over medium heat. Add the minced garlic and sauté for about 1 minute until fragrant.
2. Add the diced carrots and cook, stirring occasionally, until they are tender and lightly caramelized about 10 minutes.
3. While the carrots are cooking, place the drained and rinsed beans in a medium saucepan. Cover with water, bring to a simmer, and cook for about 5 minutes to heat through.
4. Drain the beans and add them to the skillet with the carrots. Pour in the heavy cream and stir to combine all the ingredients.
5. Cook on low heat for another 5-10 minutes, letting the mixture thicken slightly and the flavors meld. Stir frequently to prevent sticking.
6. Season the creamed beans and carrots with salt and pepper to taste. For a complete meal, serve warm as a side dish or over a bed of cooked grains like quinoa or rice.

Per serving: Calories: 250 kcal, Protein: 8 g, Carbohydrates: 30 g, Fats: 12 g, Fiber: 8 g, Sodium: Low

Chickpeas with Onion

⏰ PREP: **10 mins** ⊘ COOK: **15 mins** 🍽 SERVES: **4**

Chickpeas: 1 can (15 ounces), drained and rinsed
Onion: 1 large, thinly sliced
Olive Oil: 2 tablespoons
Garlic: 2 cloves, minced
Cumin: 1 teaspoon
Salt and Pepper: To taste

1. Heat the olive oil in a skillet over medium heat. Add the sliced onion and minced garlic. Sauté until the onion is translucent and starting to caramelize, about 8-10 minutes.
2. Stir in the drained chickpeas and cumin. Cook for another 5 minutes until the chickpeas are heated through and begin to take on some color from the pan.
3. Season with salt and pepper to taste.
4. Serve the chickpeas and onions hot. This dish can be enjoyed as is, or it can be served over rice, tucked into pita pockets, or as a topping for a salad.
5. Optionally, garnish with fresh herbs like cilantro or parsley for added flavor.
Per serving: Calories: 200 kcal, Protein: 7 g, Carbohydrates: 25 g, Fats: 8 g, Fiber: 6 g, Sodium: Low

Brussels Sprouts and Chestnuts with Thyme

⏰ PREP: **10 mins** ⊘ COOK: **25 mins** 🍽 SERVES: **4**

Brussels Sprouts: 1 pound, halved.
Chestnuts: 1 cup, cooked and peeled
Fresh Thyme: 2 tablespoons, leaves picked
Olive Oil: 3 tablespoons
Garlic: 2 cloves, minced
Salt and Pepper: To taste

1. Preheat your oven to 400°F (200°C).
2. If using fresh chestnuts, incision each chestnut and roast them in the oven until tender. Peel them once they are cool enough to handle. If using pre-cooked chestnuts, measure them out.
3. Toss the halved Brussels sprouts, peeled chestnuts, minced garlic, and fresh thyme leaves with olive oil in a large mixing bowl—season with salt and pepper to taste.
4. Spread the Brussels sprouts and chestnuts mixture evenly on a large baking sheet.
5. Roast in the preheated oven for about 20-25 minutes, stirring halfway through, until the Brussels sprouts are caramelized and the chestnuts are golden.
6. Check for seasoning, adding more salt and pepper if necessary. Serve warm as a side dish, perhaps with a sprinkle of fresh thyme leaves for garnish.
Per serving: Calories: 250 kcal, Protein: 5 g, Carbohydrates: 27 g, Fats: 15 g, Fiber: 5 g, Sodium: Low

Radicchio, Chicory, and Zucchini Gratin

⏰ PREP: **15 mins** 🔍 COOK: **30 mins** 🍽 SERVES: **4**

Radicchio: 1 head, chopped
Chicory: 1 head, chopped
Zucchini: 2 medium, sliced thinly
Heavy Cream: 1 cup
Parmesan Cheese: 1/2 cup, grated

1. Preheat your oven to 375°F (190°C).
2. Wash and chop the radicchio and chicory into bite-sized pieces. Slice the zucchini into thin rounds.
3. Combine the chopped radicchio, chicory, and sliced zucchini in a large mixing bowl.
4. Season with salt and pepper to taste. Pour the heavy cream over the vegetables and toss to coat evenly.
5. Transfer the vegetable mixture to a large baking dish, spreading out evenly.
6. Sprinkle the grated Parmesan cheese over the top of the vegetable mixture.
7. Place the baking dish in the oven and bake for about 30 minutes until the vegetables are tender and the top is golden and bubbly.

Per serving: Calories: 290 kcal, Protein: 8 g, Carbohydrates: 12 g, Fats: 24 g, Fiber: 3 g, Sodium: Low

Baked Leeks with Fennel and Potatoes

⏰ PREP: **15 mins** 🔍 COOK: **40 mins** 🍽 SERVES: **4**

Leeks: 3 large, cleaned, and cut into 1-inch pieces
Fennel Bulb: 1 large, trimmed and sliced
Potatoes: 4 medium, peeled and sliced thinly
Olive Oil: 3 tablespoons
Salt and Pepper: To taste
Thyme: 1 teaspoon dried or a few sprigs of fresh

1. Preheat your oven to 375°F (190°C).
2. After cleaning the leeks, slice them and rinse them well under running water to ensure they are free from dirt.
3. Slice the fennel bulb into thin slices similar in thickness to the potatoes.
4. Toss the leeks, fennel, and potatoes in a large mixing bowl with olive oil, salt, pepper, and thyme. Ensure all the vegetables are evenly coated.
5. Transfer the vegetable mixture to a baking dish, arranging them in an even layer for uniform cooking.
6. If using fresh thyme, tuck the sprigs among the vegetables.
7. Place the baking dish in the oven and bake for about 40 minutes until the vegetables are tender and golden brown. Stir halfway through to ensure even cooking.

Per serving: Calories: 250 kcal, Protein: 4 g, Carbohydrates: 35 g, Fats: 10 g, Fiber: 5 g, Sodium: Low

Turnips au Gratin

⏰ PREP: **10 mins** ◉ COOK: **45 mins** 🍽 SERVES: **4**

Turnips: 4 large, peeled and thinly sliced
Heavy Cream: 1 cup
Garlic: 2 cloves, minced
Gruyère Cheese: 1 cup, grated
Butter: For greasing the baking dish

1. Preheat your oven to 375°F.
2. Grease a medium baking dish with butter.
3. Arrange a layer of thinly sliced turnips at the bottom of the greased baking dish. Overlap them slightly for better structure. Sprinkle some minced garlic, salt, and pepper over the layer. Sprinkle a portion of the grated Gruyère cheese over the turnips.
4. Continue layering the turnips, garlic, salt, pepper, and cheese until all turnips are used up, finishing with a layer of cheese on top.
5. Pour the heavy cream evenly over the layered turnips. The cream will help cook the turnips and meld the layers into a cohesive gratin.
6. Cover the dish with aluminum foil and bake in the oven for 30 minutes. 7. After 30 minutes, remove the foil and continue baking for another 15 minutes or until the top is golden brown and bubbly and the turnips are tender.

Per serving: Calories: 300 kcal, Protein: 8 g, Carbohydrates: 15 g, Fats: 22 g, Fiber: 2 g, Sodium: Low

Stuffed Eggplants

⏰ PREP: **10 mins** ◉ COOK: **35 mins** 🍽 SERVES: **4**

Aubergines (Eggplants): 2 large, halved lengthwise
Ricotta Cheese: 1 cup
Spinach: 1 cup, chopped (fresh or frozen and thawed)
Parmesan Cheese: 1/2 cup, grated
Garlic: 2 cloves, minced
Olive Oil: For brushing

1. Preheat your oven to 375°F (190°C).
2. Brush the cut sides of the aubergine halves with olive oil and place them cut-side down on a baking sheet. Bake for about 20 minutes or until the flesh is tender enough to scoop out easily.
3. While the aubergines are baking, mix the ricotta cheese, chopped spinach, grated Parmesan, and minced garlic in a mixing bowl—season with salt and pepper to taste.
4. Once the aubergines are tender, remove them from the oven and carefully scoop out the flesh, leaving a thin layer to maintain the structure. Chop the scooped-out flesh and add it to the cheese and spinach mixture.
5. Spoon the filling mixture into the hollowed-out aubergine halves, mounding it slightly.
6. Place the stuffed aubergines back on the baking sheet and bake for 15 minutes or until the topping is golden and heated.

Per serving: Calories: 220 kcal, Protein: 12 g, Carbohydrates: 15 g, Fats: 13 g, Fiber: 5 g, Sodium: Low

Onions Stuffed with Spinach

⏰ PREP: **15 mins** 🔍 COOK: **40 mins** 🍽 SERVES: **4**

Large Onions: 4 (such as white or yellow onions)
Spinach: 2 cups, finely chopped (fresh or frozen and thawed)
Ricotta Cheese: 1/2 cup
Parmesan Cheese: 1/4 cup, grated
Garlic: 2 cloves, minced
Olive Oil: For brushing and sautéing

1. Preheat your oven to 350°F.
2. Peel the onions and cut off the tops. Blanch the hollowed-out onions in boiling water for 5-7 minutes to soften them. Drain and set aside to cool.
3. In a skillet, heat a tablespoon of olive oil over medium heat. Sauté the minced garlic until fragrant, about 1 minute. Add the chopped spinach and cook until the spinach is wilted and any excess moisture has evaporated.
4. Remove from heat and let it cool slightly before mixing with ricotta and half of the Parmesan cheese—season with salt and pepper to taste.
5. Stuff the blanched onions with the spinach and cheese mixture.
6. Place the stuffed onions in a greased baking dish. Brush the outside of the onions with olive oil and sprinkle the remaining Parmesan cheese on top of the stuffing. Bake in the oven for 30-40 minutes until the onions are tender and the tops are golden brown.

Per serving: Calories: 200 kcal, Protein: 8 g, Carbohydrates: 15 g, Fats: 12 g, Fiber: 3 g, Sodium: Moderate

Spelt with Turnips and Celery

⏰ PREP: **10 mins** 🔍 COOK: **45 mins** 🍽 SERVES: **4**

Spelt Grains: 1 cup, uncooked
Turnips: 2 medium, peeled and diced
Celery: 2 stalks, diced
Olive Oil: 2 tablespoons
Garlic: 2 cloves, minced
Salt and Pepper: To taste

1. Rinse the spelled grains under cold water. Bring a pot of water (about 3 cups) to a boil. Add the spelt, reduce the heat to a simmer, and cover.
2. Cook for about 40-45 minutes or until the grains are tender but still chewy.
3. Drain any excess water.
4. While the spelled is cooking, heat the olive oil in a large skillet over medium heat. Add the minced garlic and sauté for about 1 minute until fragrant.
5. Add the diced turnips and celery to the skillet. Sauté for 10-15 minutes, stirring occasionally, until the vegetables are tender and slightly caramelized.
6. Once the spelled is cooked and drained, add it to the skillet with the turnips and celery. Stir well to combine and heat through—season with salt and pepper to taste.

Per serving: Calories: 250 kcal, Protein: 8 g, Carbohydrates: 45 g, Fats: 5 g, Fiber: 8 g, Sodium: Low

Oatflakes with Spinach

⏰ PREP: **5 mins** ⏲ COOK: **15 mins** 🍽 SERVES: **4**

Oat flakes (Oatmeal): 1 cup rolled oats preferred
Fresh Spinach: 2 cups, roughly chopped
Garlic: 2 cloves, minced
Olive Oil: 2 tablespoons
Parmesan Cheese: 1/4 cup, grated
Salt and Pepper: To taste

1. Bring 2 cups of water to a boil in a pot. Add the oat flakes and a pinch of salt. Reduce the heat to low and simmer the oat flakes, stirring occasionally, until they are soft and have absorbed the water, about 10-15 minutes.
2. While the oat flakes are cooking, heat the olive oil in a skillet over medium heat. Add the minced garlic and sauté for about 1 minute until fragrant. Add the chopped spinach and cook until it wilts and reduces in volume, about 3-5 minutes. Season with salt and pepper to taste.
3. Once the oat flakes are cooked, stir them into the skillet with the spinach. Mix well to combine all the ingredients thoroughly.
4. Stir in the grated Parmesan cheese until it melts into the oat flakes and spinach mixture, adding a creamy texture and rich flavor.

Per serving: Calories: 200 kcal, Protein: 7 g, Carbohydrates: 23 g, Fats: 9 g, Fiber: 4 g, Sodium: Low

Millet with Spinach

⏰ PREP: **15 mins** ⏲ COOK: **25 mins** 🍽 SERVES: **4**

Millet: 1 cup, uncooked
Fresh Spinach: 3 cups, chopped
Onion: 1 medium, finely chopped
Garlic: 2 cloves, minced
Olive Oil: 2 tablespoons
Salt and Pepper: To taste

1. Rinse the millet under cold water using a fine mesh strainer. In a pot, bring 2 cups of water to a boil. Add the millet and a pinch of salt. Reduce the heat to low, cover, and simmer for about 20 minutes or until the water is absorbed and the millet is tender.
2. While the millet is cooking, heat the olive oil in a skillet over medium heat.
3. Add the chopped onion and minced garlic, sautéing until the onion is translucent and the garlic is fragrant about 3-4 minutes. Add the chopped spinach to the skillet. Cook until wilted and tender, about 3-5 minutes. Season with salt and pepper to taste.
4. Once the millet is cooked, fluff it with a fork and mix it into the skillet with the spinach and onions.
5. Stir everything over low heat to combine the flavors, adjusting the seasoning as needed.

Per serving: Calories: 240 kcal, Protein: 6 g, Carbohydrates: 38 g, Fats: 7 g, Fiber: 5 g, Sodium: Low

Lettuce Rolls with Millet

⏰ PREP: **15 mins** 🍳 COOK: **20 mins** 🍽 SERVES: **4**

Millet: 1 cup, uncooked
Romaine Lettuce Leaves: 8-12 large leaves, washed and dried
Carrot: 1 large, grated
Cucumber: 1 medium, julienned.
Spring Onions: 4, finely chopped
Soy Sauce: 2 tablespoons (for flavoring millet and dipping)

1. Rinse the millet thoroughly under cold water using a fine mesh strainer.
2. In a pot, bring 2 cups of water to a boil. Add the millet and a splash of soy sauce for flavor. Reduce the heat to low, cover, and simmer for about 20 minutes or until the water is absorbed and the millet is fluffy.
3. Choose large, sturdy romaine lettuce leaves which can hold the filling. Trim the stem end to make them easier to roll.
4. Prepare the carrot and cucumber by grating and julienning, respectively.
5. Chop the spring onions finely.
6. Lay a lettuce leaf flat on a clean surface. Spoon a generous amount of cooled millet onto the center of each leaf. Top the millet with grated carrot, julienned cucumber, and chopped spring onions.
7. Carefully roll the lettuce around the filling.

Per serving: Calories: 200 kcal, Protein: 6 g, Carbohydrates: 35 g, Fats: 3 g, Fiber: 4 g, Sodium: Low

Semolina Roll with Peas and Artichokes

⏰ PREP: **15 mins** 🍳 COOK: **25 mins** 🍽 SERVES: **4**

Semolina Flour: 1 cup
Milk: 2 cups
Artichoke Hearts: 1 cup, cooked and chopped (use canned or frozen, thawed)
Peas: 1/2 cup, fresh or frozen
Parmesan Cheese: 1/4 cup, grated
Olive Oil: 2 tablespoons

1. Heat the milk over medium heat in a saucepan until it starts to simmer.
2. Gradually whisk in the semolina flour, stirring constantly to avoid lumps.
3. Cook the mixture, stirring continuously, until it thickens and pulls away from the sides of the pan (about 5-7 minutes). Remove from heat and mix in the Parmesan cheese. Let the mixture cool slightly.
4. While the semolina mixture cools, heat one tablespoon of olive oil in a skillet over medium heat. Add the chopped artichoke hearts and peas, sautéing for about 5 minutes until tender—season with salt and pepper to taste.
5. On a piece of parchment paper, spread the semolina dough into a rectangular shape about 1/4 inch thick. Distribute the pea and artichoke mixture evenly over the semolina layer. Using the parchment paper to help, carefully roll the semolina dough into a log.
6. Preheat your oven to 375°F (190°C). Transfer the roll to a baking sheet, brush the outside with the remaining olive oil, and bake for 20-25 minutes or until golden and firm.

Per serving: Calories: 280 kcal, Protein: 10 g, Carbohydrates: 35 g, Fats: 12 g, Fiber: 5 g, Sodium: Low

Barley with Artichokes

⏰ PREP: **10 mins** 🍳 COOK: **40 mins** 🍽️ SERVES: **4**

Pearl Barley: 1 cup, uncooked
Artichoke Hearts: 1 cup, cooked and chopped (use canned or frozen, thawed)
Onion: 1 medium, finely chopped
Garlic: 2 cloves, minced
Olive Oil: 2 tablespoons
Salt and Pepper: To taste

1. Rinse the barley and cook in 3 cups of water with a pinch of salt. Simmer for 30-35 minutes until tender. Drain any extra water.
2. Heat olive oil in a skillet. Cook the onion for 5 minutes. Add garlic and cook for 1 minute.
3. Stir in the artichokes and cook for 5-7 minutes—season with salt and pepper.
4. Mix the cooked barley into the skillet and heat for 2-3 minutes.
5. Optionally, top with fresh herbs or Parmesan.

Per serving: Calories: 250 kcal, Protein: 6 g, Carbohydrates: 40 g, Fats: 8 g, Fiber: 8 g, Sodium: Low

Brown Rice Ring with Wild Mushrooms

⏰ PREP: **10 mins** 🍳 COOK: **25 mins** 🍽️ SERVES: **4**

1 cup brown rice, uncooked
1 cup wild mushrooms, sliced
1 onion, finely chopped
2 tablespoons olive oil
2 cloves garlic, minced
Salt and pepper to taste

1. Cook the brown rice according to the package instructions. Set aside.
2. Heat olive oil in a skillet over medium heat. Add the onion and garlic, cooking until softened, about 5 minutes. Add the wild mushrooms and sauté for 5-7 minutes until tender. Season with salt and pepper.
3. Mix the cooked rice with the sautéed mushrooms.
4. Press the mixture into a greased ring mold or bundt pan, then invert onto a plate.

Per serving: Calories: 250 kcal, Protein: 5 g, Carbohydrates: 40 g, Fats: 8 g, Fiber: 4 g, Sodium: Low

Buckwheat with Apples, Radishes, & Cheese

⏰ PREP: **10 mins** ⌚ COOK: **10 mins** 🍽 SERVES: **4**

1 cup sprouted buckwheat
1 apple, chopped
Four radishes, thinly sliced
1/2 cup Emmenthal cheese, diced
2 tablespoons olive oil
Salt and pepper to taste

1. Rinse the sprouted buckwheat under cold water. If you prefer it warm, lightly steam it for 5 minutes. Otherwise, use it as is.
2. Mix the buckwheat with the chopped apple, sliced radishes, and diced Emmenthal cheese in a bowl.
3. Drizzle with olive oil and season with salt and pepper. Toss to combine.
4. Serve immediately as a light meal or side dish.

Per serving: Calories: 220 kcal, Protein: 7 g, Carbohydrates: 25 g, Fats: 10 g, Fiber: 5 g, Sodium: Low

Briam

⏰ PREP:**50mins** ⌚ COOK:**1h.30mins** 🍽 SERVES:**4**

2 large potatoes, sliced
2 zucchinis, sliced
1 large eggplant, sliced
2 ripe tomatoes, chopped
1/2 cup olive oil
Salt and pepper to taste

1. Preheat your oven to 375°F (190°C).
2. Slice the potatoes, zucchini, and eggplant. Chop the tomatoes.
3. Place all the vegetables in a large baking dish. Drizzle with olive oil and season generously with salt and pepper. Toss to coat the vegetables evenly.
4. Cover the baking dish with aluminum foil and bake for 1 hour. Remove the foil and continue baking for 30 minutes until the vegetables are tender and slightly browned.
5. Serve the brim hot as a main dish or side.

Per serving: Calories: 230 kcal, Protein: 3 g, Carbohydrates: 28 g, Fats: 13 g, Fiber: 5 g, Sodium: Low

DESSERTS

Stewed Apples with Saffron

⏰ PREP: **10 mins** 🔍 COOK: **20 mins** 🍽 SERVES: **4**

Four large apples, peeled, cored, and sliced
1/4 cup honey (or sugar, if preferred)
1/4 teaspoon saffron threads
1/2 cup water
1 tablespoon lemon juice
Pinch of salt

1. Soak the saffron threads in 2 tablespoons of warm water for about 5 minutes to release their color and flavor.
2. In a saucepan, combine the sliced apples, honey (or sugar), and saffron with soaking water, lemon juice, water, and a pinch of salt.
3. Bring to a simmer over medium heat, stirring gently.
4. Cover and cook for 15-20 minutes or until the apples are tender but still hold their shape. Stir occasionally to prevent sticking.
5. Serve warm as a dessert, topped with yogurt or ice cream, or as a side dish for roasted meats.

Per serving: Calories: 130 kcal, Protein: 5 g, Carbohydrates: 38 g, Fats: 7 g, Fiber: 16 g, Sodium: Low

Raspberries in Syrup

⏰ PREP: **5 mins** 🔍 COOK: **10 mins** 🍽 SERVES: **4**

2 cups fresh raspberries
1/2 cup sugar
1/4 cup water
1 teaspoon lemon juice

1. Combine the sugar, water, and lemon juice in a saucepan. Heat over medium heat, stirring until the sugar dissolves.
2. Gently add the raspberries to the saucepan. Simmer for 5-7 minutes, stirring occasionally, until the raspberries release their juices and the mixture thickens slightly.
3. Remove from heat and let the raspberries cool. They can be served warm or chilled.
4. Transfer to a jar or container and refrigerate for up to a week.

Per serving: Calories: 100 kcal, Protein: 0.5 g, Carbohydrates: 25 g, Fats: 0 g, Fiber: 4 g, Sodium: 0 mg

Sage Sorbet

🕐 PREP: **10 mins** 🍳 COOK: **5 mins** 🍽 SERVES: **4**

1 cup fresh sage leaves, loosely packed
1 cup sugar
2 cups water
Two tablespoons lemon juice
Pinch of salt

1.Combine the sugar, water, and salt in a saucepan. Bring to a simmer over medium heat, stirring until the sugar dissolves.
2. Add the sage leaves and continue to simmer for 5 minutes. Remove from heat and let it steep for 15-20 minutes.
3. Strain the sage leaves from the syrup and discard the leaves. Stir in the lemon juice.
4. Let the syrup cool to room temperature, then transfer it to the refrigerator to chill for at least 1 hour.
5. Pour the chilled syrup into an ice cream maker and churn according to the manufacturer's instructions. Alternatively, pour the mixture into a shallow container and freeze, stirring every 30 minutes to break up ice crystals until smooth.
6. Scoop the sorbet into bowls and garnish with fresh sage leaves if desired.
Per serving: Calories: 140 kcal, Protein: 0 g, Carbohydrates: 36 g, Fats: 0 g, Fiber: 0 g, Sodium: 10 mg

Ricotta Pots with Raspberries

🕐 PREP: **10 mins** 🍳 COOK: **10 mins** 🍽 SERVES: **4**

1 cup ricotta cheese
Two tablespoons honey (or sugar, if preferred)
1/2 teaspoon vanilla extract
1 cup fresh raspberries
One tablespoon chopped nuts (optional for topping)
Mint leaves (optional for garnish)

1. Combine the ricotta cheese, honey, and vanilla extract in a bowl. Mix well until smooth and creamy.
2. Divide the ricotta mixture evenly into four small serving pots or bowls. Top each pot with a handful of fresh raspberries.
3. Sprinkle chopped nuts on top for some added crunch, and garnish with mint leaves if desired.
4. Serve immediately or refrigerate for 30 minutes to chill before serving.
Per serving: Calories: 180 kcal, Protein: 6 g, Carbohydrates: 15 g, Fats: 10 g, Fiber: 2 g, Sodium: 50 mg

Greek Yogurt with Honey and Walnuts

⏰ PREP: **5 mins** 🔍 COOK: **5 mins** 🍽 SERVES: **4**

1 cup Greek yogurt
2 tablespoons honey
1/4 cup walnuts, chopped
A pinch of cinnamon (optional)

1. Spoon the Greek yogurt into a serving bowl.
2. Drizzle the honey over the yogurt.
3. Sprinkle the chopped walnuts on top.
4. Add a pinch of cinnamon for extra flavor if desired.
5. Serve chilled as a refreshing and healthy dessert.

Per serving: Calories: 300 kcal, Protein: 12 g, Carbohydrates: 34 g, Fats: 15 g, Fiber: 2 g, Sodium: 60 mg

Orange & Almond Cake

⏰ PREP: **10mins** 🔍 COOK: **2h.30mins** 🍽 SERVES: **4**

3 oranges
3 cups almond flour
1 cup sugar
3 eggs
1 teaspoon baking powder

1. Preheat your oven to 350°F (175°C) and grease a 9-inch cake pan.
2. Boil two oranges (unpeeled) in water for about two hours until soft, then blend into a puree.
3. Mix the almond flour, sugar, and baking powder in a bowl.
4. Add the eggs and orange puree to the dry ingredients and mix until smooth.
5. Pour the batter into the prepared cake pan.
6. Bake for 45-50 minutes or until a toothpick inserted into the center comes clean.
7. Cool and serve with slices of the remaining fresh orange.

Per serving: Calories: 320 kcal, Protein: 10 g, Carbohydrates: 40 g, Fats: 16 g, Fiber: 5 g, Sodium: 150 mg

Baked Figs with Ricotta

⏰ PREP: **10 mins** 🍳 COOK: **25 mins** 🍽 SERVES: **4**

6 fresh figs, halved
1/2 cup ricotta cheese
2 tablespoons honey
A few sprigs of fresh thyme

1. Preheat your oven to 350°F (175°C).
2. Arrange the fig halves on a baking sheet and cut side up.
3. Spoon a small amount of ricotta cheese onto each fig half.
4. Drizzle honey over the figs and ricotta.
5. Bake in the oven for 10-15 minutes or until the figs are soft and warm.
6. Garnish with fresh thyme before serving.

Per serving: Calories: 180 kcal, Protein: 5 g, Carbohydrates: 30 g, Fats: 5 g, Fiber: 3 g, Sodium: 45 mg

Poached Pears

⏰ PREP: **10 mins** 🍳 COOK: **10 mins** 🍽 SERVES: **4**

4 pears, peeled, halved, and cored
4 cups water
1 cup sugar
2 cinnamon sticks
1 vanilla pod, split lengthwise (or 1 teaspoon vanilla extract)

1. Combine water, sugar, cinnamon sticks, and the vanilla pod in a large saucepan over medium heat.
2. Bring to a simmer and stir until the sugar dissolves.
3. Add the pear halves and simmer gently for 15-20 minutes or until the pears are tender.
4. Remove the pears with a slotted spoon and reduce the syrup by simmering for 10-15 minutes.
5. Serve the pears with a drizzle of the reduced syrup.

Per serving: Calories: 200 kcal, Protein: 0.5 g, Carbohydrates: 51 g, Fats: 0 g, Fiber: 4 g, Sodium: 5 mg

Rice Pudding with Raisins

🕐 PREP: **10 mins** 🍳 COOK: **25 mins** 🍽 SERVES: **4**

1/2 cup white rice (short-grain or medium-grain)
4 cups milk
1/4 cup sugar
1/2 cup raisins
1 teaspoon vanilla extract
1/2 teaspoon cinnamon (optional, for garnish)

1. Combine the rice and 2 cups of milk in a medium saucepan. Bring to a simmer over medium heat, stirring frequently.
2. Once the milk is mostly absorbed, add the remaining 2 cups of milk, sugar, and raisins. Continue to cook on low heat, stirring often, for about 20-25 minutes or until the mixture thickens and the rice is tender.
3. Remove from heat and stir in the vanilla extract.
4. Spoon the rice pudding into bowls and sprinkle with cinnamon if desired. It can be served warm or chilled.

Per serving: Calories: 250 kcal, Protein: 6 g, Carbohydrates: 45 g, Fats: 5 g, Fiber: 1 g, Sodium: Low

Whole Wheat Ring Cake with Yogurt

🕐 PREP: **10 mins** 🍳 COOK: **30 mins** 🍽 SERVES: **4**

1 1/2 cups whole wheat flour
1 cup plain yogurt
3/4 cup sugar (or honey for a natural sweetener)
1/2 cup olive oil (or any neutral oil)
2 eggs
1 1/2 teaspoons baking powder
1 teaspoon vanilla extract (optional)
Pinch of salt

1. Preheat your oven to 350°F. Grease a ring (Bundt) cake pan with oil or butter.
2. Whisk together the yogurt, sugar, eggs, olive oil, and vanilla extract in a large bowl until smooth.
3. Combine whole wheat flour, baking powder, and salt in a separate bowl. Gradually add the dry ingredients to the wet mixture, stirring until combined.
4. Pour the batter into the greased ring cake pan and spread evenly.
5. Bake in the oven for 30-35 minutes or until a toothpick inserted into the center comes clean.
6. Allow the cake to cool in the pan for 10 minutes before transferring to a wire rack to cool completely.
7. Slice and enjoy!

Per serving: Calories: 250 kcal, Protein: 5 g, Carbohydrates: 33 g, Fats: 11 g, Fiber: 2 g, Sodium: Low

Oranges Filled with Fruit Salad

⏰ PREP: **10 mins** 🍳 COOK: **5 mins** 🍽️ SERVES: **4**

4 large oranges
1 cup strawberries, diced
1 cup blueberries
1 kiwi, peeled and diced
1 apple, diced
Two tablespoons honey (optional for sweetness)
Mint leaves for garnish (optional)1/2 teaspoon baking soda

1. Slice the top off each orange and carefully hollow out the interior using a spoon.
2. Reserve the orange segments and remove any seeds. Trim a small portion from the bottom of each orange shell if necessary to help them stand upright without rolling.
3. Combine the reserved orange segments, diced strawberries, blueberries, diced kiwi, and chopped apple in a bowl.
4. Drizzle honey over the fruit mixture and gently toss to combine and coat evenly. The honey not only adds sweetness but also helps to meld the flavors together.
5. Spoon the fruit salad mixture back into the hollowed-out orange shells.

Per serving: Calories: 150 kcal, Protein: 2 g, Carbohydrates: 35 g, Fats: 0.5 g, Fiber: 6 g, Sodium:

Mediterranean-Style Chocolate Cake

⏰ PREP: **10 mins** 🍳 COOK: **30 mins** 🍽️ SERVES: **4**

1 1/2 cups all-purpose flour
1/2 cup unsweetened cocoa powder
1 cup sugar
1/2 cup extra virgin olive oil
3/4 cup Greek yogurt (plain)
3 eggs
1 teaspoon baking powder
1/2 teaspoon baking soda
Zest of 1 orange

1. Preheat the oven to 350°F. Grease a cake pan (8-inch round or Bundt pan) with olive oil and dust with flour.
2. Sift the flour, cocoa powder, baking powder, baking soda, and salt.
3. Whisk together the sugar, olive oil, Greek yogurt, eggs, and orange zest in a separate bowl until smooth.
4. Gradually add the dry ingredients to the wet mixture, stirring until combined.
5. Pour the batter into the prepared pan and bake for 30-35 minutes, or until a toothpick inserted into the center comes out clean.
6. Let the cake cool in the pan for 10 minutes before transferring to a wire rack to cool completely.
7. Optionally, dust with powdered sugar or drizzle with melted dark chocolate before serving.

Per serving: Calories: 350 kcal, Protein: 6 g, Carbohydrates: 42 g, Fats: 18 g, Fiber: 3 g, Sodium: 120

Little Cheese Envelopes with Honey

⏰ PREP: **15 mins** ◎ COOK: **20 mins** 🍽 SERVES: **4**

One package of phyllo dough (or puff pastry), thawed
1 cup ricotta cheese (or any soft cheese like goat cheese or cream cheese)
Honey, for drizzling
One egg, beaten (for egg wash)
Butter melted (for brushing phyllo)

1. Preheat your oven to 375°F (190°C). Line a baking sheet with parchment paper.
2. Lay out one sheet of phyllo dough on a clean surface. Brush lightly with melted butter. If you're using puff pastry, roll it out slightly and cut into squares (about 4x4 inches). Place a small spoonful of cheese in the center of each square.
3. Fold the dough over the cheese diagonally to form a triangle, or bring all corners together at the top if using squares. Pinch the edges to seal.
4. Gently brush the outside of each envelope with a beaten egg to help it turn golden when baked.
5. Arrange the cheese envelopes on the prepared baking sheet. Bake for 15-20 minutes or until golden and puffed. Once baked, remove the envelopes from the oven and immediately drizzle with honey while still warm.

Per serving: Calories: 150 kcal, Protein: 4 g, Carbohydrates: 15 g, Fats: 8 g, Fiber: 0.5 g, Sodium: Low

Fresh Walnut Spoon Sweet

⏰ PREP: **10 mins** ◎ COOK: **2 hours** 🍽 SERVES: **4**

1 pound fresh green walnuts (young walnuts, if available)
1 cup raw sugar
2 cups water
1 lemon, juice and zest
1 cinnamon stick
Cloves (optional, 3-4 cloves for flavor)

1. Pierce each walnut a few times with a needle or a small knife. This helps the syrup penetrate the walnuts.
2. Soak the pierced walnuts in water for five days, changing the water daily to remove bitterness.
3. Combine honey, water, lemon juice, lemon zest, and the cinnamon stick in a large pot. Bring to a boil, then reduce to a simmer.
4. Drain the walnuts from the soaking water and add them to the boiling syrup. Add cloves if using.
5. Simmer the mixture gently for about 1-2 hours or until the walnuts are tender and the syrup has thickened.
6. Let the walnuts cool in the syrup. Once cool, transfer them to sterilized jars. Pour the thickened syrup over the walnuts, ensuring they are completely covered. Seal the jars and store them in a cool, dark place.
7. They can be enjoyed immediately but improve with age.

Per serving: Calories: 180 kcal, Protein: 2 g, Carbohydrates: 40 g, Fats: 5 g, Fiber: 1 g, Sodium: Low

Fried Semolina Diamonds

⏰ PREP: **10 mins** 🍳 COOK: **15 mins** 🍽️ SERVES: **4**

1 cup semolina
1/2 cup sugar (for dough and syrup)
1/2 teaspoon ground cardamom
Water (enough to make a dough and syrup)
Oil for frying
One teaspoon of lemon juice (for syrup)

1. Mix 1/4 cup sugar with 1/2 cup water in a small saucepan and bring to a boil. Reduce heat and simmer until slightly thickened, about 5-7 minutes.
2. Stir in lemon juice, remove from heat, and set aside to cool.
3. Combine the semolina, 1/4 cup sugar, and cardamom in a bowl. Gradually add water, mixing until a firm dough forms.
4. Roll out the dough on a clean surface to about 1/4 inch thickness. Cut into diamond shapes using a knife.
5. Heat oil in a deep frying pan over medium heat. Carefully place the diamond cuts in the hot oil and fry until golden brown, flipping once. Remove from oil and drain on paper towels.
7. While still hot, dip the fried diamonds into the prepared syrup for a few seconds, then remove them and allow them to cool on a wire rack.

Per serving: Calories: 250 kcal, Protein: 3 g, Carbohydrates: 40 g, Fats: 7 g, Fiber: 1 g, Sodium:

Plum and Cinnamon Jam

⏰ PREP: **10 mins** 🍳 COOK: **35 mins** 🍽️ SERVES: **4**

4 cups plums, pitted and chopped
2 cups sugar
1/4 cup lemon juice
One teaspoon ground cinnamon
1/2 teaspoon vanilla extract (optional, if not counting as an ingredient)

1. Wash the plums, remove the pits, and chop them into small pieces.
2. Combine the chopped plums, sugar, and lemon juice in a large saucepan.
3. Bring the mixture to a boil over medium heat, stirring frequently to dissolve the sugar. Once boiling, reduce the heat to low and simmer gently. Add the ground cinnamon and stir to incorporate.
4. Simmer for about 20-25 minutes until the jam has thickened and the plums are very soft. Mash the plums slightly with a spoon if you prefer a smoother texture.
5. If using, stir in the vanilla extract just before turning off the heat.
6. Place a small spoonful of jam on a cold plate. If it gels and doesn't spread much when tilted, it's ready.
7. Sterilize jars and lids according to safe canning guidelines. Fill the hot, sterilized jars with the hot jam, leaving about 1/4-inch headspace. Wipe the rims clean, place the lids on the jars, and tighten the bands.
8. Process the jars in a water bath canner for 10 minutes (adjusting for altitude as needed).

Per serving: Calories: 50 kcal, Protein: 0 g, Carbohydrates: 13 g, Fats: 0 g, Fiber: 0 g, Sodium: 0 mg

28-Day Meal Plan

Shopping List Week 1

Proteins:
Eggs (for Harissa Shakshuka, Tortilla Espanola, quiche)
Lamb (for two dinners), Chickpeas (canned or dry, for salads and breakfast), Sausage (for dinner), Shrimp (for Garlic Shrimp Spaghetti), Scallops (for Easy Carbonara), Pork chops (for dinner)
Chicken (for quiche), Salmon (for dinner)

Dairy:
Yogurt (for Eggplant & Yogurt Parfait and Muesli), Skyr (for Muesli), Ricotta cheese (for Savory Ricotta), Tahini (for Cobb Salad dressing), Heavy cream (for lamb with cream)
Cheese (Parmesan for Carbonara, and any other cheeses for salads and garnishes)

Vegetables:
Harissa paste , Mixed greens (for Cobb Salad and Chopped Med Salad)
Artichokes (canned or fresh)
Eggplants (for Simple Eggplant Mold and Eggplant & Yogurt Parfait), Garlic, Onions
Green peas (fresh or frozen), Kale (for dinner with shrimp)
Cabbage, Zucchini (for noodle salad), Butternut squash
Bell peppers, tomatoes, and other vegetables for salads and the quiche

Fruits:
Lemons (for various recipes)
Grapes (for roasted sausage dish)
Apples, bananas, and any other preferred fruits for breakfast or as snacks
Grains and Nuts:
Couscous (for breakfast)
Phyllo dough (for Lamb with Cream)
Pasta (for spaghetti and carbonara)
Polenta (for Roasted Sausage dinner)
Muesli
Pistachios (for Savory Ricotta)
Various nuts (for breakfast and salads)
Seasonings and Oils:
Olive oil, Balsamic vinegar
Spices (including cardamom, cumin, coriander, cinnamon, etc.)

The Meal Plan Week 1

	Breakfast	Lunch	Dinner
Mon.	Harissa Shakshuka	Cobb Salad with Roasted Chickpeas & Creamy Tahini Dressing	Lamb with Artichokes, Egg, and Lemon
Tues.	Chopped Med Salad with Crispy Chickpeas	Simple Eggplant Mold	Roasted Sausage and Grapes with Polenta
Wed.	Tortilla Espanola	Green Pea Soup	Lamb with Cream Wrapped in Phyllo
Thurs.	Eggplant & Yogurt Parfait	Savory Ricotta with Pistachios	Garlic Shrimp Spaghetti with Buttery Kale
Fri.	Muesli with Skyr	Cabbage with Balsamic Vinegar	Easy Carbonara with Scallops and Peas
Sat.	Fruit & Nut Couscous	No-Pasta Zucchini Noodle Salad	Roasted Butternut Squash and Pork Chops
Sun.	Grain-Free Chicken & Vegetable Quiche	Cream of Cucumber Soup	Spice Salmon

Shopping List Week 2

Produce:
Blueberries (for smoothie)
Green peas (for soup), Garlic, Kale
Zucchini (for noodle salad)
Pumpkin (for pudding)
Fresh herbs (like parsley, basil for various dishes)
Amaretto biscuits (or almond-flavored cookies)
Lemons (for various recipes and salad dressings)
Eggplants, Butternut squash
Broccoli rabe, Scallions, Cucumbers
Mixed greens (for salads)
Bell peppers, onions, and tomatoes (for omelette and quiche)
Artichokes (canned or fresh if available)

Proteins:
Shrimp, Lamb (for two dinners), Pork chops, Scallops, Chicken (for quiche), Salmon, Prosciutto (for oat salad), Eggs (for omelette, quiche, and other dishes)

Dairy:
Milk or a milk alternative (for smoothies and porridge)
Ricotta cheese (for savory snack)
Parmesan cheese (for carbonara and salads), Heavy cream (for lamb with cream), Butter
Grains and Nuts:
Amaretto biscuits (or substitute)
Quinoa (for porridge)
Chia seeds (for porridge)
Oats (for breakfast salad)
Phyllo dough (for lamb with cream), Polenta (for roasted sausage dish), Pistachios

Seafood:
Shrimp, Scallops, Salmon
Spices and Seasonings:
Amaretto (liqueur for the pudding, optional), Spices such as salt, pepper, nutmeg, cinnamon, Olive oil
Vinegars (for dressings and sautéing)
Lemon juice

Miscellaneous:
Honey or a sweetener of choice (for smoothies and porridge)
Coffee or tea (if desired for breakfast)

The Meal Plan Week 2

	Breakfast	Lunch	Dinner
Mon.	Blueberry Cheesecake Smoothie	Green Pea Soup	Garlic Shrimp Spaghetti with Buttery Kale
Tues.	Pumpkin and Amaretto Biscuit Pudding	No-Pasta Zucchini Noodle Salad	Lamb with Cream Wrapped in Phyllo
Wed.	Quinoa and Chia Porridge	Simple Eggplant Mold	Roasted Butternut Squash and Pork Chops
Thurs.	Green Morning Smoothie	Sautéed Broccoli Rabe Salad	Easy Carbonara with Scallops and Peas
Fri.	Fruit & Oat Salad with Crispy Prosciutto	Savory Ricotta with Pistachios	Roasted Sausage and Grapes with Polenta
Sat.	Mediterranean Omelette	Vegan Nicoise Salad	Lamb with Artichokes, Egg, and Lemon
Sun.	Grain-Free Chicken & Vegetable Quiche	Cream of Cucumber Soup	Spice Salmon

Shopping List Week 3

Produce:
Trout (smoked), Mixed greens (for salads), Fresh dill, Zucchini, Butternut squash, Cucumbers, Eggplants, Kale
Tomatoes (for wraps and skewers)
Bell peppers (for wraps)
Chickpeas (canned or dry if preparing from scratch)
Artichokes (canned or fresh)
Garlic, Lemons
Pistachios, Grapes
Green peas
Onions (various, for multiple dishes)
Halloumi cheese (for skewers)
Dairy & Eggs:
Yogurt (plain, for salads and parfait)
Heavy cream
Eggs
Parmesan cheese (for eggplant mold)
Ricotta cheese
Proteins:
Pork chops, Shrimp, Salmon, Lamb (for two dishes)
Mussels, Chorizo
Pantry Staples:
Olive oil
Balsamic vinegar
Tahini
Various spices (including dill, salt, pepper, and specialty spices for the "Spice Salmon" and other dishes)
Chicken or vegetable broth (for soups)
Phyllo dough
Rice (for paella)
Granola (or ingredients to make your own)
Nuts for granola and salads
Herbs & Seasonings:
Fresh herbs (such as parsley, basil, mint, depending on your taste and recipe needs)
Ground spices like cumin, coriander, paprika (especially for Mediterranean and spiced dishes)
Additional Items:
Bread or tortillas for breakfast wraps
Honey or other sweeteners

The Meal Plan Week 3

	Breakfast	Lunch	Dinner
Mon.	Smoked Trout Breakfast Salad with Creamy Dill Dressing	No-Pasta Zucchini Noodle Salad	Roasted Butternut Squash and Pork Chops
Tues.	Cucumber & Herb Yogurt Salad	Simple Eggplant Mold	Garlic Shrimp Spaghetti with Buttery Kale
Wed.	Mediterranean Breakfast Wraps	Cobb Salad with Roasted Chickpeas & Creamy Tahini Dressing	Lamb with Artichokes, Egg, and Lemon
Thurs.	Mediterranean Omelette	Savory Ricotta with Pistachiosse	Roasted Sausage and Grapes with Polenta
Fri.	Earthy Granola	Green Pea Soup	Spice Salmon
Sat.	Eggplant & Yogurt Parfait	Cream of Cucumber Soup	Lamb with Cream Wrapped in Phyllo
Sun.	Grilled Tomato and Halloumi Skewers	Cabbage with Balsamic Vinegar	Squash Rice Paella with Mussels & Chorizo

Shopping List Week 4

Produce:
Smoked salmon, Onions (for pickling and various dishes)
Cucumbers (for soup and salads)
Grapes, Tomatoes, Halloumi cheese
Eggplants
Lettuce and mixed greens, (Chickpeas (canned or dried, if preparing from scratch)
Artichokes (canned or fresh), Lemons, Zucchini, Peaches
Fresh mint, Broccoli rabe, Butternut squash

Dairy & Eggs:
Eggs (for crepes, omelette, and carbonara)
Yogurt (plain for parfait and salad dressing)
Ricotta cheese, Cottage cheese
Parmesan cheese (for spaghetti and carbonara)
Heavy cream (for lamb dish)

Meat & Seafood:
Smoked salmon
Sausage, Shrimp, Lamb (for two dishes), Scallops
Pork chops

Pantry Staples:
Flour (for crepes), Polenta, Olive oil
Balsamic vinegar, Tahini
Pasta (for spaghetti)
Rice or pasta for carbonara (depending on your recipe)
Chicken or vegetable broth Herbs,

Spices & Condiments:
Salt and pepper
Various dried herbs and spices (such as dill, cumin, coriander, paprika, etc.)
Pickling ingredients (such as vinegar, sugar, salt)

Optional:
Nuts (pistachios for the ricotta dish)
Bread or tortillas (for wraps)
Honey or other sweeteners (if preferred for enhancing flavors or breakfasts)
Special Items:
Halloumi cheese (for skewers)

The Meal Plan Week 4

	Breakfast	Lunch	Dinner
Mon.	Blender Crepes with Smoked Salmon & Quick-Pickled Onions	Cream of Cucumber Soup	Roasted Sausage and Grapes with Polenta
Tues.	Grilled Tomato and Halloumi Skewers	Cabbage with Balsamic Vinegar	Garlic Shrimp Spaghetti with Buttery Kale
Wed.	Eggplant & Yogurt Parfait	Cobb Salad with Roasted Chickpeas & Creamy Tahini Dressing	Lamb with Artichokes, Egg, and Lemon
Thurs.	Cucumber & Herb Yogurt Salad	Savory Ricotta with Pistachios	Easy Carbonara with Scallops and Peas
Fri.	Mediterranean Breakfast Wraps	Green Pea Soup	Garlic Shrimp Spaghetti with Buttery Kale
Sat.	Mediterranean Omelette	No-Pasta Zucchini Noodle Salad	Lamb with Cream Wrapped in Phyllo
Sun.	Cottage Cheese with Sliced Peaches and Fresh Mint	Sautéed Broccoli Rabe Salad	Roasted Butternut Squash and Pork Chops

Bonus Gift!
Complimentary E-Book for Healthy Eating Lovers!

Hello, health enthusiasts!
As a heartfelt thank you for being part of our healthy eating community, I'm thrilled to offer you a special bonus: a complimentary e-book titled "Mediterranean Diet Cookbook for Beginners" .
This guide is packed with:
Essential tips to get started on the Mediterranean diet
Simple, delicious recipes that are easy to make at home
Nutritional insights to help you make balanced food choices
Meal plans tailored for beginners, designed to boost your energy and well-being

Index

Made in the USA
Monee, IL
31 December 2024

75768818R00059